HOOKED RUG
TREASURY

Jessie A. Turbayne

Schiffer Publishing Ltd

4880 Lower Valley Road, Atglen, PA 19310 USA

Dedication

This book is dedicated to Annie A. Spring, rug
hooking artist, teacher, and friend.

Rug hooking artist and teacher Annie A. Spring hooked "Such-a-
Mola" using a combination of hand-dyed woolen yarns and fabrics.
The design was adapted from the colorful clothing worn by Kuna
women living off the coast of Panama on the San Blas Islands. Jane
Flynn pattern. 1996. 22" x 33". *Courtesy of Annie A. Spring.*

Library of Congress Cataloging-in-Publication Data

Turbayne, Jessie A.
   Hooked rug treasury/Jessie A. Turbayne.
      p. cm.
   Includes bibliographical references.
   ISBN 0-7643-0301-5 (hardcover)
   1. Rugs, Hooked--United States. I. Title.
NK2812.T87 1997
746.7'4'0973--DC21   97-24250
                                 CIP

Designed by "Sue"

ISBN: 0-7643-0301-5
Printed in China

Title page photo: This very effective antique rug of twin bouquets
was worked primarily in earth tones. Added touches of red, white,
and blue enhance the floral displays. 1860-1880. 49" x 67". *Courtesy
of Ledlie I. Laughlin Jr.*

Published by Schiffer Publishing Ltd.
4880 Lower Valley Road
Atglen, PA 19310
Phone: (610) 593-1777; Fax: (610) 593-2002
E-mail: Schifferbk@aol.com
Please write for a free catalog.
This book may be purchased from the publisher.
Please include $3.95 for shipping.

In Europe, Schiffer books are distributed by
Bushwood Books
84 Bushwood Road
Kew Gardens
Surrey TW9 3BQ England
Phone: 44 (0)181 948-8119; Fax: 44 (0)181 948-3232
E-mail: Bushwd@aol.com

Please try your bookstore first.
We are interested in hearing from authors
with book ideas on related subjects.

Table of Contents

This handsome, radiating star hooked rug would be the focal point of any room. Late nineteenth century. 41" x 41". *Courtesy of Country Braid House.*

Acknowledgements

I wish to express my sincere gratitude to the many whose contributions made this book a reality. Those who shared their time, ideas, and rugs were family members, friends and associates, collectors, rug hookers, rug hooking teachers, antique dealers, shop, gallery, and auction house owners, museums, and historical societies. A very special word of appreciation to my readily available and always helpful editors, Nancy Schiffer and Tina Skinner.

I wish to thank Joel Tobey, who generously gave of his time. It was a delight to hear him recall the stories of Molly Nye Tobey, the mother he dearly loved and rug hooking artist I have long admired.

I am grateful to Bill Fidalgo in whose hands the contents of William Winthrop Kent's Cape Cod summer home now rests. Mr. Fidalgo kindly allowed me to photograph the collection of hooked rugs, supplied vintage photographs and graciously shared William Winthrop Kent's story as told to him by Kent's daughter, Charlotte.

To Susan Logue, I truly appreciate the assistance you gave in helping me research some of Canada's finest rug hookers.

Thank you to Jeanie Crockett Ritchie, who took time from her busy schedule and shared with me her literary talents and much needed humor.

Thank you to Susan Smidt for being an endless source of rug hooking information and memorabilia.

To my brother Jamie, who twenty-four years ago suggested I start restoring hooked rugs and has helped me ever since, I thank you.

To Annie A. Spring, to whom I have dedicated this book, thank you for making me part of your illustrious rug hooking heritage.

Last but not least, thank you to Michael and Rob, who, by sharing my life, share in its seemingly endless chaos.

Kind acknowledgements to Dot Abbott; Betsy Adams; Mike Adams; Antiques and Art, Portsmouth, New Hampshire; The Association of Traditional Hooking Artists; Jasmine Benjamin; Jeanne Benjamin; Elizabeth Black; Anne Boissinot; Marilyn Bottjer; Braid-Aid, Pembroke, Massachusetts; Richard Breneman; D. Marie Bresch; Hollis Brodrick Antiques; Claudia and Steve Brown; Charles and Adair Burlingham; Mary Sheppard Burton; former President and Mrs. George Bush; The Butler-Silverman Collection; The Cahoon Museum of American Art, Cotuit, Massachusetts; Elaine Cathcart; Sandra Cheverie, George Christ Collection; Catherine Clay; Collins Auction Galleries, Kennebunk, Maine; Caroline Eshbach Cornish; Country Braid House, Tilton, New Hampshire; Linda Rae Coughlin; Verna Cox; Gloria E. Crouse; Patrice Crowley; Jane Curtin; W. Cushing and Company, Kennebunkport, Maine; Jeremiah Dalton House Antiques, Wiscasset, Maine; Catherine Detwiller; DiFranza Designs, North Reading, Massachusetts; Colette Donovan, Merrimacport,
Massachusetts; C. Lois Dugal; Eastern Massachusetts Corvette Club; Elizabeth Enfield/Mount Vernon Antiques, Rockport, Massachusetts; the family of Barbara Whitehouse Eshbach; Robert D. Farwell; Jeanne Fields; Fruitlands Museums, Harvard, Massachusetts; Robert and Meredith Gammons; Susan Folk Gilkey; Russ and Karen Goldberger, Hampton, New Hampshire; Elizabeth T. Green; Constance Greer Antiques; Jacqueline Denizard Gutting; Fumiyo Hachisuka; Hallie Hall; Sue Hammond; Frank Hanchett; Dan and Jodi Harris; Patricia Haviland; Peg Irish; Esther R. Jackson; The Barbara Johnson Collection; Thomas Johnson; Jean L. Jones; Kaminski Auctioneers and Appraisers, Stoneham, Massachusetts; Francoise Labbe; Ledlie I. Laughlin Jr.; Paula and Bill Laverty; Roslyn Logsdon; Ramona Maddox; Bettina Drake Maraldo; Charlene Marsh; Prudence R. Matthews; Robert L. Matthews; Betty McClentic; Anna B. McCoy; The McGown Guild; Pat Merikallio; Chris Merryman; Marie Miller; Kathleen M. Moriarty; Dr. and Mrs. John B. Morrison; Joan Moshimer; Paul Moshimer; Robert Moshimer; The Ontario Hooking Craft Guild; Rafael Osona; Amy Oxford; The Oxford Company, Middlebury, Vermont; Kim Nelson; Marjorie Noon; The Old York Historical Society, York, Maine; Robert Alexander Petta; Martha V. Pike; Shirley Poole; Janet Stanley Reid; Florence Richardson-Rich, Ralph Ridolfino; Olga Rothschild; *Rug Hooking* magazine; Margaret Ruhland; Michael Santos; Ann Sargent; Gordon and Susan Scale; Robert Schleck; Loretta M. Schuster; Stephen Score Inc, Boston, Massachusetts; Jan Seavey/Rising Hawk Studio; Phylis Sexton; Virginia Sheldon; Trudi Shippenberg; Jule Marie Smith; Patricia Smith; Betsy Snel; The Society for the Preservation of New England Antiquities, Boston, Massachusetts; Peter Stec; Terri Strack; Joan M. Stocker; Elizabeth A. Supple; Meredith Pride Swan; Joel Nye Tobey; Jonathan Starbuck Tobey; Joshua Ashley Tobey; Anthony and Florence Travis; C. Allan Turbayne; Evelyn N. Turbayne; James A. Turbayne; Stephen A. Turbayne; Leah Christine Runci-Valerie; Marcy Van Roosen; Kitsie Von Santos III; Waioli Mission House-Grove Farm Homestead, Kauai, Hawaii; Robin Moore Walker; Anne V. Wallace; Carolyn Arrington-Watt; Theresa J. Wells; Donald and Sally (Gammons) Wheeler; Shirley Wiedemann; Ann Winterling; Jane Workman; Jamie Wyeth; and Nancy Zuese.

Hooked rug measurements have been rounded to the nearest inch. Height precedes width. Ages assigned to the rugs have been supplied by their owners or are to the best of my knowledge. All rugs are hooked on burlap unless otherwise noted. In some cases of special interest, the hooking materials have been listed. Those hooked rugs, mats, and related items to which no acknowledgement has been ascribed belong to the author.

Introduction

Red acanthus leaf scrolls complement a colorful floral pattern. Note
the single cluster of grapes among the blooms and foliage. This fine
example of a late-nineteenth-century hooked hearth rug awaits
restoration. 1870-1890. 32" x 53".

Tuesday, October 22, 1996, 4:20 A.M.

The hooked rug on the table is more than a hundred
years old and has visibly suffered from decades of neglect.
Geometrical patterns of calico cloth are peppered with
holes; the edges are ragged and torn; once-bright wool flowers have faded with time. Before the sun rises, my day
begins much as it has for the last twenty-odd years, by
mending old hand-hooked rugs. Bringing damaged rugs
back to their former glory is a labor of love for me.

By the time rays of the morning sun appear to keep
me company, I have completed nearly two hours of hand
sewing, forming and hiding tiny linen stitches in between
hooked loops of century-old paisley. With the aid of natural light, the task begins of selecting and dyeing fabrics to
match those the rug has long lost. Scraps of homespun
wool and cotton rag litter the floor. Steam begins to rise
from a boiling pot of dye.

An unexpected yet pleasant break in the morning oc-
curs when friend and fellow antique dealer Florence Travis
arrives at my door, precariously balancing her famous apple
pie in one hand and grasping two hooked rugs in the other.
Behind follows husband Anthony, toting a half dozen more
hole-ridden rugs. The visit is an enjoyable one, combining

business, lunch, and pleasure, but typically their
time with me is all too brief.

UPS delivers, telephones continue to ring, and
the afternoon sun has dried the morning-dyed selection of old and new materials. Strips of cotton
rag, carefully cut into quarter-inch widths, are
worked into a reinforced burlap foundation. Carefully I place the new cotton loops, dyed to look
old, beside those hooked a hundred years before.
The rug demands four more hours of attention;
stitching and hooking, I continue to work. Before
long the sun sets, natural light is gone, and outside
the studio window the sky is as it was at 4:20 A.M.

Noteworthy or not, old or new, all hooked rugs
share the common bond of beginning with hand
and hook. The process of pulling fabric strips,
yarns, or twine up through a woven base to form
raised loops has remained the same throughout the
craft's history. What has changed in the past twenty
years is the degree of appreciation that people, other
than antique dealers and collectors, have for the
rugs that I have spent my adult life repairing. Ex-
posure in popular magazines, increased use by interior decorators, greater interest among textile and

folk art enthusiasts, and growth of the rug hooking community have all contributed to bringing to the attention of the general public the aesthetic and monetary values of hand-hooked rugs. Due to this relatively new regard, restoration services are in greater demand and the need to start my workday before the sun rises has become a necessity.

However, this book does not deal with the recently gained popularity of, or much overdue respect for, a select group of floor textiles. After years of handling countless hooked rugs, I was asked to compile a visual inventory of those I considered memorable. And though this project has been more than twenty years in the making, the task has been a pleasurable one. From the most dedicated hands and from the most passionate collectors, I present to you this treasury of the choicest hooked rugs, antique and modern.

Jessie A. Turbayne

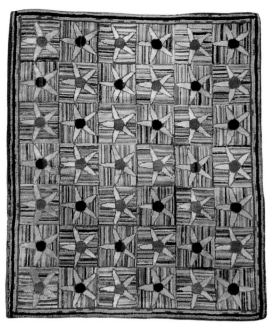

Stars dance upon a hit-or-miss basket-weave background. 1910-1930. 39" x 47".

Detail of a hit-or-miss design hooked rug. Dated 1883 and in need of repair. *Courtesy of Sidney and Elizabeth Stewart.*

Handsome in every respect, this area-size rug of traditional scroll and floral pattern was hooked in rich earth tones with accents of red. The center floral motif is raised and sculptured. 1870-1890. 6' 1" x 7'. *Courtesy of Antiques and Art.*

Life in the country seems to agree with this contented cat. Early twentieth century. 24" x 38". *Private Collection.*

1. What's Desirable in Hooked Rugs

From the late 1980s through the mid '90s, my brother Jamie and I participated in a variety of New England antique shows. From standing ankle deep in mud at outdoor flea markets, to sampling paté at posh affairs, we did them all. Regardless of the show's pedigree or the collector's budget, I was continually asked for certain types of hooked rugs. What follows is a sampling of those most requested.

A rug maker's tools: fabrics and well-worn hook.

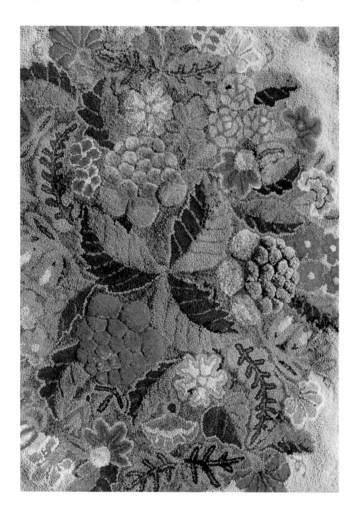

Detail of a choice floral patterned, area-size hooked rug with raised and sculptured cabbage roses. 1870-1890. *Courtesy of Antiques and Art.*

This fine example of an early hooked hearth rug was found in pristine condition on Cape Cod in Massachusetts. 1850-1870. 30" x 69". *Courtesy of Russ and Karen Goldberger.*

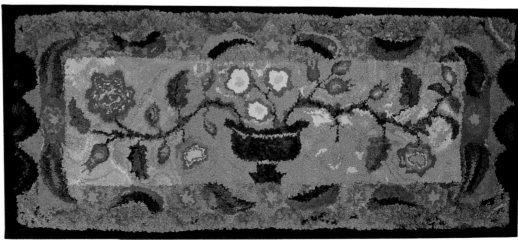

Rugs on Linen

Burlap, in the form of sacking, was first introduced in North America during the 1850s. Used for transporting feed and grain, the jute woven sacks, when washed and cut open, made an ideal base for hooking rugs. Prior to the use of burlap, some rugs were hooked on a variety of homespun foundations. Linen, spun and woven from flax plants that were commonly grown on farms during the early 1800s and known for its durability, was the choice of some rug makers. Hooked rugs on linen of this vintage are uncommon.

Detail shows the top surface and underside of hooked rug on linen.

An exceptional example of an early floral hooked rug on linen features cabbage roses in various stages of bloom. The maker worked with woolen materials and yarns and a variety of homespun cotton fabrics. 1850-1870. 30" x 48". *Courtesy of Country Braid House.*

A well-designed and skillfully hooked early rug on linen. Homespun cotton and woolen fabrics and yarns were used by the rug maker. 1850-1870. 29" x 50". *Courtesy of Colette Donovan.*

Red curlicue scrolls frame a simplistic spray of mixed flowers. Woolen fabrics hooked on a linen foundation. 1870-1890. 26" x 48".

Due to a general ban on representational art, few Shakers hooked pictorial rugs. This simple depiction of a moose, framed with a bold block border, was made by Shakers living within the Shirley, Massachusetts, community (1793-1909). Hooked on burlap using a variety of fabrics, including cotton jersey. 1870-1890. 45" x 36". *Courtesy of the Fruitlands Museums.*

Shaker-made Hooked Rugs

"Do all your work as though you had a thousand years to live, and as you would if you knew you must die tomorrow."—Mother Ann Lee

Shaker Society was based upon principles of balance, order, and isolation, with the ideology that men and women were separate but equal. Founder Mother Ann Lee, an English factory worker who believed herself to be the female manifestation of Christ, came to America in 1774 with eight devoted followers and the desire to create a utopian world. Despite opposition and hardships, the celibate sect grew. By the mid-1840s, members numbered almost six thousand with eighteen communities in Massachusetts, New Hampshire, Connecticut, Maine, New York, Kentucky, Indiana, and Ohio.

Shaker men, women, and the children brought into the Society were assigned daily chores. They worked and lived together in large multilevel houses, "brothers" on one side, "sisters" on the other. The floors in these community houses were often covered with a wide assortment of rugs. Among the varieties were woven, braided, crocheted, knitted, sewn, hooked, and hooked-types. The majority of the hooked rugs were crafted by the "sisters" in the late 1800s and, unlike other Shaker products, were made only for use within the community and not for sale to the "outside world." Well designed and skillfully executed, the hooked rugs were pleasing to the eye, and could be quite colorful, but following the sect's general ban on representational art, few were pictorial. Abstract and geometric designs were common, though some generic floral patterns were hooked. During the early 1900s, linoleum was widely used by the Shakers, resulting in the need for fewer handmade floor coverings.

The number of practicing Shakers dropped dramatically during the post–Civil War Industrial Revolution and have continued to do so. The Shaker Society's current membership has dwindled to but a few.

Because of their exceptional designs and fine craftsmanship, Shaker-made products are highly regarded and sought after by collectors. Unfortunately, the term "Shaker made" has been attached to some unauthentic items, including hooked rugs.

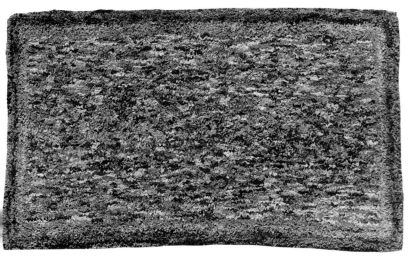

A simple pattern of uniformly spaced black lines separate hit-or-miss stripes. This hooked rug on burlap was purchased at auction and reported to be Shaker made. Woolen braids surround the rug. 1920-1940. 31" x 42". *Courtesy of the Butler-Silverman Collection.*

A multicolored abstract design, framed with shades of olive, was hooked on burlap using woolen and cotton fabric strips. Tops of the hooked loops were clipped giving this rug its shaggy appearance. Attributed to the Shakers. 1890-1910. 35" x 59". *Courtesy of the Butler-Silverman Collection.*

Below: Borders within borders frame an "eye-catching" oval configuration. Mixed materials on burlap. Attributed to the Shakers. Possibly of Kentucky origins. 1900-1920. 36" x 49". *Courtesy of the Butler-Silverman Collection.*

Pictured is a Shaker-made rug that was crafted with knitting needles, heavy knitting cotton, and short woolen and cotton fabric scraps each measuring about 1 1/2" long. As the "sister" knit, the scraps were worked into the stitches. Knitted pieces, complete with bits of fabric, were sewn together forming a rug. The top surface of the finished rug resembles that of hooked work on burlap but the foundation and technique used are very different from traditional hooking. Rugs made in this manner are often referred to as hooked-types though no hook was used. 1870-1890. 15" x 32".

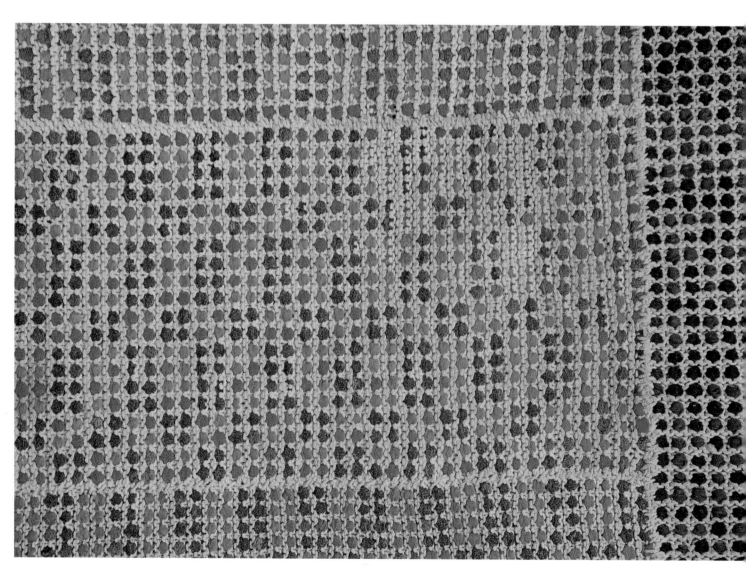

This underside detail of the aforementioned hooked-type rug shows
the knitted foundation upon which the rug was worked.

Hooked and Braided Rugs

Braided rugs were first seen in North American homes during the early 1800s. Frugal needleworkers fashioned braids from yardage of fabric, scraps of material, and discarded clothing. Three or more strips of cloth were plaited to form rope-like lengths. These lengths were then sewn or laced together creating long-wearing, warm, and often colorful carpets.

Rugs hooked on a burlap base appeared in the same regions from the mid-1800s on. Braids were sometimes sewn along a rug's perimeter; the braided buffer prolonged the life of the somewhat more fragile hooked interior. When a hooked rug was damaged beyond repair, some creative homemakers preserved a section of intact hooking and surrounded it with braids.

Today there is a renewed interest among contemporary rug makers for the pleasing and durable combination of hooked and braided rugs.

Hooked blooms, buds, and foliage are framed by concentric rectangles and braided borders. 1870-1890. 22" x 36". *Collection of Sidney and Elizabeth Stewart.*

A hooked background complements colorful braided circles. 1890-1910. 53" x 34". *Courtesy of Hollis Brodrick Antiques.*

Three rows of braiding frame a hooked center motif of scroll and peacock tail design. 1880-1890. 35" x 52". *Private Collection.*

Detail shows the border of sturdy braids that protect and decorate a less durable hooked interior.

This hooked design of an elongated star surrounded by a zigzag frame was edged with rows of braiding. 1920-1940. 26" x 32". *Courtesy of Country Braid House.*

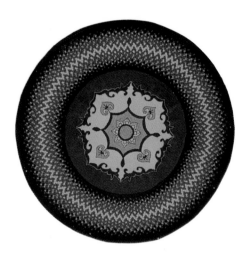

Complementary braids enhance "Sandakan," a Ginny's Gems design. Hooking by Hope Camp. Braiding by Sandra Cheverie. 1965. Diameter 45". *Courtesy of Braid-Aid.*

A braided rug of bold design frames a finely hooked center of fruit and foliage. Diameter 8' 5". Center motif was hooked in the 1970s. Braided area was recently made by Country Braid House. *Courtesy of Country Braid House.*

"Westport Flowers" is a harmonious blend of hooking and braiding. Designed by Hook Nook. Hooked and braided by Sandra Cheverie. 1988. 20" x 36". *Courtesy of Braid-Aid.*

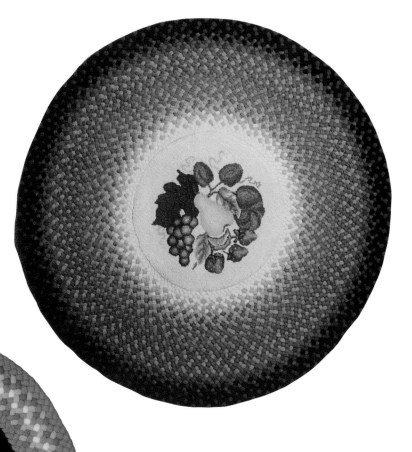

Color-coordinating braids and hooked fruit motif combine to make an appealing rug. Hooking by Joan Dwyer. Braiding by Country Braid House. 1990. Diameter 36". *Courtesy of Country Braid House.*

Braids of blue, olive, and white echo the shades found in a hooked wreath of morning glories. The floral pattern was designed by Joan Moshimer and hooked by Polly Merrill. Braiding by Verna Cox. 1994. Diameter 23". *Courtesy of Verna Cox and Joan Moshimer.*

Fur, Feather, Fins, and Friends

The most sought after of all hooked rugs are those depicting animals. The rug hooker's personal interpretation of creatures large and small is often nostalgic and whimsical, making animal hooked rugs appealing to a wide variety of collectors.

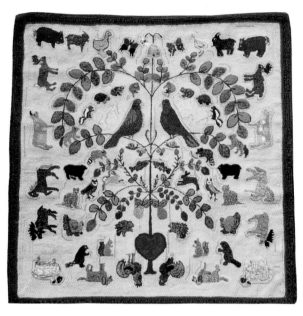

A menagerie of creatures large and small enhance a symmetrical tree of life design. 1994. 54" x 54". Designed and hooked by Betsy Adams. *Courtesy of Betsy Adams.*

Words of wisdom from a prolific cat on the prowl. 1880-1900. 84" x 48". *Courtesy of Elizabeth Enfield/Mount Vernon Antiques.*

Misplaced eyes add a whimsical note to an otherwise ordinary cat. 1870-1890. 20" x 36". *Private Collection.*

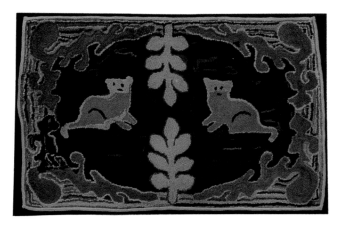

Simplistic cats of similar coloring but different markings are separated by stalk-like branches of foliage. Note the crude scroll that frames the pair. 1870-1890. 27" x 43". *Private Collection.*

One tail up and one tail down; black cats pose on a hit-or-miss stripe background. 1910-1930. 28" x 44". *Private Collection.*

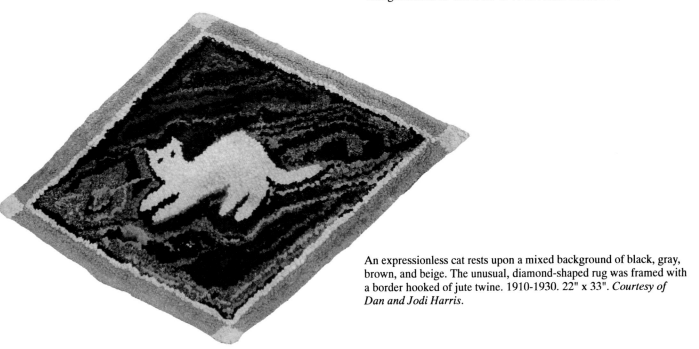

An expressionless cat rests upon a mixed background of black, gray, brown, and beige. The unusual, diamond-shaped rug was framed with a border hooked of jute twine. 1910-1930. 22" x 33". *Courtesy of Dan and Jodi Harris.*

Kathryn Lehman was born on December 27, 1909, in Thomas Mills, Pennsylvania. She died on September 20, 1994, and was laid to rest in a small Mennonite church cemetery near her Somerset County home. This portrait of a startled black cat was hooked in the 1950s during Miss Lehman's engagement then placed in a hope chest for safekeeping. Her fiance died and the rug never left the chest until it was sold at an auction in Davidsville, Pennslyvania, in 1995. 27" x 44". *Courtesy of the George Christ Collection.*

A pensive Siamese cat watches a playful butterfly. 1975. 14" x 14". *Courtesy of DiFranza Designs.*

"Max and Sushi," designed and hooked by Pat Merikallio. A very satisfied cat is surrounded by his swimming supper. 1992. 25" x 40". *Courtesy of Pat Merikallio.*

A bewildered white cat sits beside a basket of folk art flowers. 1994. 18" x 34". *Courtesy of DiFranza Designs.*

Posed against an abstract picket fence, this cat and dog take time to play. 1910-1930. 30" x 48". *Courtesy of Elizabeth Enfield/ Mount Vernon Antiques.*

The image of a beloved pet dog was framed with a meandering vine of simple flowers and buds. Mixed materials on burlap. 1850-1870. 25" x 36". *Courtesy of Ralph Ridolfino.*

This design of the reclining dog was copied from a popular Edward Sands Frost (1843-1894) hooked rug pattern. The rug maker took the liberty of replacing Frost's preprinted background motif with darting birds, blooming flowers, and a very un-Frost-like border. 1870-1890. 26" x 47". *Private Collection.*

A delightful hooked likeness of a Boston terrier rests upon a series of colorful backdrops. 1920-1940. 29" x 40". *Courtesy of Dr. and Mrs. John B. Morrison.*

Lush, vibrant foliage surrounds a realistic depiction of "Toby," a rug designed and hooked by Pat Merikallio. 1995. 42" x 47". *Courtesy of Pat Merikallio.*

Ready for action, this dog was carefully posed against an abstract landscape. The rug maker has framed the hooked work with a complementary abstract border. 1930-1950. 28" x 53". *Courtesy of Jane Workman.*

Below: "Millie and Ranger in Maine" depicts Millie (the author of *Millie's Book* which she dictated to her loving mistress Barbara Bush) and her son, Ranger who was President Bush's dog. They are shown at the Bush's summer home surrounded by beach roses and the rocks and waves of the Atlantic Ocean. Barbara Bush commissioned rug hooking artist and author Joan Moshimer of Kennebunkport, Maine, to design and hook this portrait of the Bush's beloved pets. "Millie and Ranger in Maine" will eventually be placed in George Bush's Presidential Library at Texas A & M University. 1997. 26" x 47". *Courtesy of President and Mrs. George Bush.*

Three-leaf clovers and eight-pointed stars are suspended around a primitive folk art horse. 1860-1880. 22" x 39". *Courtesy of Charles and Adair Burlingham.*

Two primitive horses stand nose to nose in a near mirror image. 1890-1910. 18" x 36". *Courtesy of Colette Donovan.*

"Weather Wise" features words of wisdom and a horse caught in mid-gallop. 1985. 25" x 32". *Courtesy of DiFranza Designs.*

The black sheep of the flock heads in another direction. 1989. 24" x 36". *Courtesy of DiFranza Designs.*

This scene from a real-life farmyard soap opera was captured with wool and hook by Betsy Adams. 1995. 31" x 52". *Courtesy of Betsy Adams.*

A proud rooster with chevroned plumage struts across a dark background. 1910-1930. 21" x 39". *Courtesy of Dan and Jodi Harris.*

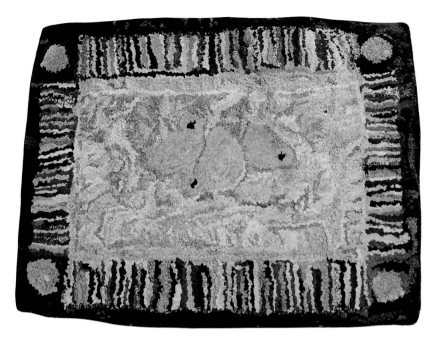

Three baby chicks peck for grain atop a mottled field. 1915-1935. 28" x 37". *Courtesy of Betsy Adams.*

A lively mirror image of birds, flowers, and scrolls. 1910-1930. 27" x 41". *Private Collection.*

Two herons are depicted in their natural habitat. Patterns formed by trailing vines and the placement of light colors against dark combine to create the effect of a stained glass window. 1940s. 36" x 26". *Courtesy of the George Christ Collection.*

Twin bunnies decorate a late-nineteenth-century hooked motto rug. Signed 1896. 33" x 37". *Courtesy of Russ and Karen Goldberger.*

The outlined shape of a reclining deer rests on a primitive woodland landscape. 1910-1930. 19" x 34". *Private Collection.*

A bold and kingly lion springs forth. 1870-1890. 30" x 45". *Courtesy of Stephen Score Inc.*

Vibrant red blooms frame a diminutive prancing tiger. 1900-1920. 25" x 37".

Elizabeth Black's hooked pillow portrait of a tiger's face mimics the exactness of a photograph. 1994. 20" x 20". *Courtesy of Elizabeth Black.*

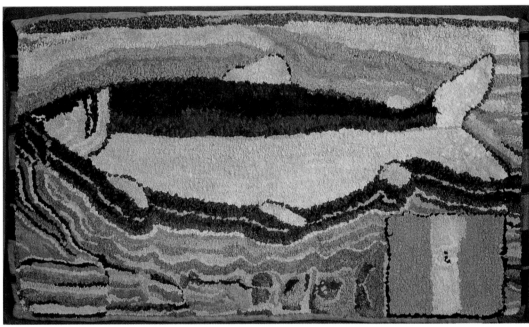

An unusual hooked replica of a trophy fish with "Fly Book" inscription. Coastal Maine origins. 1890s. 21" x 36". *Courtesy of Russ and Karen Goldberger.*

A realistic rainbow trout makes its way over a rocky bed in cold northern waters. Designed and hooked by Susan Folk Gilkey. 1995. 28" x 36". *Courtesy of Susan Folk Gilkey.*

Pictured is the Oxford punch needle used by hooking artists such as Meredith Pride Swan. The tool is threaded with yarn and then poked down through a woven foundation. Raised loops are formed on the underside of the design. *Courtesy of the Oxford Company.*

Photographs from the *Island Journal*, used in conjunction with an article focusing on cod fishing in Newfoundland and Labrador, inspired Meredith Pride Swan to pay homage to the catch of young and old fisherfolk. The Oxford punch needle (a technique somewhat different from traditional rug hooking) and hand-dyed woolen yarns were used to create the rug. 1995. 30" x 46". *Courtesy of Meredith Pride Swan.*

Anne Wallace upholstered her favorite wing chair with a menagerie of folk art animals that she designed and hooked. 1995. *Courtesy of Anne V. Wallace.*

This rug of four flounders was designed by Meredith Pride Swan as a group project to raise money for a community scholarship program at the Lincoln School in Providence, Rhode Island. Eighteen mothers and students, using the Oxford punch needle and woolen yarns, worked on the pattern while in school. Two thousand dollars was realized in a raffle for the rug. 1996. 42" x 63". *Courtesy of Meredith Pride Swan.*

Silent Companions

For those who appreciate animal hooked rugs but are undecided whether they should be placed on the floor or hung upon the wall, imaginative rug hookers have created hooked silent companions.

Hooked in memory of a beloved companion, "Sam" silently stands guard outside the door of his owner and creator, Terri Strack. 1992. 30" x 22". *Courtesy of Terri Strack.*

"The tiger is an animal of mystery and surprise, appearing suddenly and dramatically, then disappearing under cover as secretly as it arrived. The tiger inspired me to hook this piece, not only because they are beautiful and intriguing, but because the memories of their history beckoned me. I lived in Pakistan shortly after the era of the raj, when the big tiger shoots were the sport of the rajahs and the British rulers. Although these cats are dangerous to men and very much feared, I felt regretful of their endangerment." The silent companion "Tigris" (the Latin spelling for a female tiger in poetry, not prose) was designed and hooked by artist Ann Winterling. 1990. 22" x 42". *Courtesy of Ann Winterling.*

"Collie Pup," designed and hooked by Elizabeth Black, is cute and cuddly but, unlike its living counterpart, requires none of the work. 1990. 20" x 18". *Courtesy of Elizabeth Black.*

Frisky "Wirehaired Terrier Pup" is ready to play. Designed and hooked by Elizabeth Black. 1991. 18" x 22". *Courtesy of Elizabeth Black.*

Two-legged Friends

Always pleasing and sometimes poignant, hooked rugs that depict people are desirable but hard to come by.

Dressed in warm winter attire, two female figures toss crumbs into the air for awaiting yellow birds. This charming hooked mat was given to Roberta Wales when she was child by distant relative Mrs. Nellie Burnham. From the original collection of Ralph W. Burnham, early twentieth century "Hooked Rug Magnate" of Ipswich, Massachusetts. 1890-1910. 19" x 35".

Rowing in waters hooked of jute twine, two sailors watch a passing steamer. Possibly of Canadian origins. Early twentieth century. 21" x 35". *Private Collection.*

With a sense of humor and a satirical twist, rug hooker Frank Hanchett has captured the memorable moment when "Eve Shows Adam the Big Apple." 1996. 40" x 32". *Courtesy of Frank Hanchett.*

"One's Life Lived on Earth as It Is in Heaven" was designed and hooked by Linda Rae Coughlin. 1996. 48" x 34". *Courtesy of Linda Rae Coughlin.*

2. By the same Hand—The Makers

Hooked rugs fashioned by the same hand have not always remained with their maker. Tattered and torn, past their days of household serviceability, hooked rugs were often relegated to shelter the woodpile. Those that survived were commonly dispersed to friends and family, their provenance lost along the way. Complete and intact collections worked by one person, now prized and sought after, are rare indeed.

Antique Trio

Two of the hooked rugs pictured were purchased by this author during the early 1990s at the Brimfield Antique Market in Brimfield, Massachusetts. Several years later, antique dealer Colette Donovan of Newburyport, Massachusetts, sent a similar rug to my studio for restoration. Upon close examination of design elements, foundations, fabrics, and hooking technique, it was easily determined that the trio of mid-nineteenth-century hooked rugs were made by one hand. Separated by an unknown amount of time and distance, the rugs were once again united.

Bold bloom, bud, and leaf design of mellow color is enhanced by added touches of red. Hooked on a homespun foundation. Mid nineteenth century. 67" x 68".

Below: Flower buds, blossoms, and leaves are borne on slender stalks which radiate from a central bloom. Hooked on a homespun foundation. Mid nineteenth century. 41" x 61".
Courtesy of Colette Donovan.

A center cluster of seven blossoms is framed by pairs of leaves, flower buds, and additional blooms. Hooked on a homespun foundation. Mid nineteenth century. 45" x 53".

The rug maker who hooked these three floral patterns most likely drew and cut out a template for each motif: bloom, bud, and leaf. The template was then placed on the homespun foundation and traced. Design elements could be interchanged, creating a variety of interpretations.

Waioli Mission House and Grove Farm Homestead

Between 1820 and 1848 the American Board of Commissioners for the Foreign Missions, a voluntary organization founded in Boston, sent one hundred and eighty Protestant men and women to the Hawaiian Islands in hopes of spreading Christianity. In 1846, missionaries Abner Wilcox and his wife, Lucy, sailed to Kauai, leaving behind their teaching positions in rural Connecticut. The life of the missionary family was a busy one, for they acted as ministers, teachers, builders, doctors, nurses, and parents. The Wilcoxes occupied a wooden frame house built in 1836 under the direction of the Reverend William Alexander and known as Waioli Mission House. Decorated with furnishings brought from New England and those crafted by island cabinetmakers, Waioli House would be home to three missionary families for more than thirty years. The Wilcoxes were in residence from 1846 to 1869; four of their eight children were born there.

After 1850, the role of the missionaries began to change. The Hawaiian church became self-sufficient, resulting in decreased intervention from the American Board in Boston. Rules governing the lives of those brought to the islands were relaxed. Missionaries previously prevented by the Board from buying Hawaiian lands were allowed to do so. The majority of the Board's land holdings were granted to missionaries who remained in Hawaii. The Wilcoxes continued to live at the Waioli Mission House until 1869. During a visit to the "Eastern States" that same year, Abner and Lucy were exposed to malaria while riding the transcontinental train. Both died in Connecticut.

Wilcox family members still in Hawaii kept the Waioli House, but by the early 1900s the property had seriously begun to deteriorate. Lucy Etta Wilcox Sloggett, Elsie Wilcox, and Mabel Wilcox, granddaughters of Abner and Lucy, purchased the Mission House, which underwent extensive repair and refurbishment in 1921. During the summer of 1922 Miss Elsie and Miss Mabel sailed to New England in search of appropriate period furnishings for the Mission House. In addition to vintage furniture given by Wilcox relatives in Connecticut, the two sisters went shopping for antiques in New York, Vermont, Maine, and Massachusetts as well as Connecticut. Pur-

chases of furniture, a spinning wheel, and hooked rugs were crated and shipped home to Hawaii.

Grove Farm on the east coast of Kauai was acquired in 1864 by George Wilcox, one of the seven children of missionaries Abner and Lucy Wilcox. The sugar plantation, which grew to include the family house, several cottages, office, and wash house, was home to the well-to-do bachelor until his death at age 93 in 1933. At that time the plantation was inherited by his nieces and nephews. In order to preserve the family homestead, Miss Mabel purchased Grove Farm in 1970, which under her guidance became a nonprofit museum to be enjoyed by the people of Kauai.

Waioli Mission House was incorporated as a historic house museum in 1952 with family members acting among the board of directors. Miss Elsie died in 1954. Miss Mabel continued to enjoy life on the island until her death in 1978 at the age of ninety-six. According to her wishes, Grove Farm Homestead Museum was willed to the people of Kauai.

Hooked rugs brought from New England and New York by Miss Mabel and Miss Elsie in 1922 can still be found at Waioli Mission House and at Grove Farm Homestead. Over the past few years, I have had the privilege of working with Robert Schleck, curator for Grove Farm Homestead and Waioli Mission House, on a project to restore some of the hooked rugs in the museums' collection. Two of the rugs that arrived at my studio from balmy Hawaii during the height of a blinding New England snowstorm bore whimsical marks of their maker. In the corner of each rug a small and simple face was hooked. With careful examination of technique, design, foundations, and fabrics, I felt confident that these two rugs dating from the latter half of the nineteenth century were hooked by the same hand. And that their maker was not only talented at rug hooking but possessed a sense of humor.

Waioli Mission House—Hanalei, Kauai, Hawaii—1927. Reprinted with the permission of Robert Schleck. From his book, *The Wilcox Quilts in Hawaii.* 1986. Senda Photo. *Courtesy of Robert Schleck.*

Toward the end of the 1970s, the late Barbara Eshbach, popular rug hooking teacher and lecturer from Schenectady, New York, was commissioned by the curator of the Waioli Mission House to reproduce two hooked rugs that had been damaged beyond repair. Pictured is the Mission House first-floor bedroom of Abner and Lucy Wilcox with the faithfully hooked replicas in place. *Courtesy of the family of Barbara Whitehouse Eshbach.*

An anonymous rug maker left his or her mark (a small face) on this hooked mat interrupting an otherwise common hit-or-miss pattern. Purchased by Miss Mabel Wilcox. Believed to be of New England origins. Late nineteenth century. 17" x 26". *Courtesy of Grove Farm Museum.*

Detail of the rug hooker's mark.

Pictured above is one of the damaged rugs that was sent to my studio for repair. The rug maker's mark appears in the form of a small hooked face. Purchased by Miss Mabel Wilcox. Believed to be of New England origins. Late nineteenth century. 37" x 54". *Courtesy of Grove Farm Museum.*

Detail of the rug hooker's mark.

Restored to its former glory, this hooked rug combines the maker's own hit-or-miss-style border with a traditional floral center often seen on preprinted hooked rug patterns popular during the late 1800s. Late nineteenth century. 37" x 54". *Courtesy of Grove Farm Museum.*

Whimsical Settings and Such

During the 1960s, Ann Sargent purchased part of a collection of early twentieth century New Hampshire–made hooked rugs from an antique dealer in Northwood, New Hampshire. Knowing her daughter's desire to own the complete grouping, Ann's mother returned to the shop and bought the remaining rugs. She presented them as a gift to her daughter one Christmas. The hooked rugs have been in Ann's possession ever since.

Childlike scenes with primitive block letters depict historical buildings in and about the Portsmouth, New Hampshire, area. Also included in the collection are a Nantucket cottage, reclining cat, Liberty Bell, eagle-like bird with Latin verse, as well as other unidentified structures.

The array of hooked rugs bear no identifying marks or signature of the maker. Nor are there any visible dates of when or indication of where they were made. From the information given to Ann Sargent by the dealer who sold the collection and through close visual examination one can be confident that the rugs were crafted by the same hand. Hooking style and technique are consistent in all nineteen rugs. Each was hooked on a burlap base using a grab bag variety of wide-cut strips; some of these fabric strips are distinctive enough to be recognized in a number of the rugs.

An unusual looking structure documented "Jackson House 1664 Portsmouth. HH." Early twentieth century. 32" x 22". *Courtesy of Ann Sargent.*

Depiction of what is believed to be a Portsmouth, New Hampshire, Navy yard ship house. Early twentieth century. 25" x 35". *Courtesy of Ann Sargent.*

Hooked replica of a stately church supposedly in the Portsmouth, New Hampshire, area. Marked with the dates 1703-1818. Early twentieth century. 24" x 39". *Courtesy of Ann Sargent.*

Was "Jaffary" the owner of this salt box–style home or was the rug maker perhaps referring to Jaffrey, New Hampshire? Early twentieth century. 26" x 37". *Courtesy of Ann Sargent.*

Unidentified commercial-looking structure inscibed "16 60 Richard.Cutt". Early twentieth century. 27" x 39". *Courtesy of Ann Sargent.*

Unidentified house marked "J:Reed 1700". Early twentieth century. 25" x 41". *Courtesy of Ann Sargent.*

A bare, twig-like tree stands guard beside a simple dwelling. Did the home belong to someone of the name Atkinson? Or was the house located in Atkinson, New Hampshire? Early twentieth century. 22" x 35". *Courtesy of Ann Sargent.*

Multi-windowed building sports the word "Pepperell" across its twin-chimneyed roof. Pepperell is a Massachusetts town near the New Hampshire border, but could also be the owner of the rather impressive-looking structure. The meaning of "New. March" is unknown to this author. Early twentieth century. 22" x 33". *Courtesy of Ann Sargent.*

A misspelled tribute to Robert Burns (1759-1796), Scottish poet born in the parish of Alloway in Ayrshire. By honoring such a scholarly poet one begins to wonder if the maker of these primitive looking rugs was truly naive or just skillful at the art of deception. Early twentieth century. 34" x 34". *Courtesy of Ann Sargent.*

The first letter of this inscription was lost when the rug's corner was damaged. " RYER FROST" remains. Perhaps the cryptic message pays homage to American poet Robert Frost (1874-1963), who for the first five years of the 1900s pursued his farming interests in Derry, New Hampshire. From 1905 to 1911, Frost taught English at Derry's Pinkerton Academy. Early twentieth century. 24" x 33". *Courtesy of Ann Sargent.*

Were Walton, Bell, Lock, and Davidson part of a list of favored literary figures? Or just plain folk who resided in this house? Early twentieth century. 27" x 38". *Courtesy of Ann Sargent.*

Two unidentified neighboring homes documented "White. Allen." Early twentieth century. 22" x 39". *Courtesy of Ann Sargent.*

A jumble of letters (note the backward N's which also appear in other rugs in the collection) and misspelled words make it difficult to decipher this rug's motto. When corrected it would read, "Those pleasant days of old that so often people praise—A Lobster Man's Home". Early twentieth century. 28" x 40". *Courtesy of Ann Sargent.*

One can imagine happy (and smelly) times at "V C Rands Fish House." The location of Hoskins Point remains a mystery. Early twentieth century. 22" x 37". *Courtesy of Ann Sargent.*

Perhaps the rug maker visited Nantucket during the warm days of summer when cottage doors and window shutters were left open. Early twentieth century. 22" x 32". *Courtesy of Ann Sargent.*

An unrecognizable house documented "Washingtoh New Yorkes." Early twentieth century. 25" x 39". *Courtesy of Ann Sargent.*

A crudely rendered cat with oversized ears reclines in its box-like bed. Early twentieth century. 25" x 36". *Courtesy of Ann Sargent.*

The wording "Liberty Bell" identifies an already recognizable national symbol. Early twentieth century. 26" x 36". *Courtesy of Ann Sargent.*

A primitive eagle-like bird hovers between two Latin phrases, "E Pluribus Unum," "Out of many, one," and "Nil Desprandum" [sic], "Never despair." Early twentieth century. 27" x 37". *Courtesy of Ann Sargent.*

Molly Nye Tobey

Molly Nye Tobey was a woman of the '90s long before the expression entered our vocabulary. Born May 9, 1893, she lived her ninety-one years to the fullest, leaving behind a legacy rich in family, friends, and international admirers. With an abundance of spirit and determination, she successfully managed a career and home at a time when most women were expected to chose one or the other. Mrs. Tobey was a respected artist the rug hooking world will long remember and often recall.

Born Mary Nye Gammons in New Bedford, Massachusetts, Molly, as she preferred to be addressed, spent girlhood days on a two-hundred-acre farm surrounded by

the wildlife and flowers that would later influence her artwork and design skills. Of her New Bedford school years, she recalled, "I reached high school and was fortunate in having a very fine instructor in stenciling, metal enameling, and weaving. My teacher at high school was a dear old friend of Helen Albee, who had started the Abnakee Rug Industry in New Hampshire, and so in 1907, I started with Helen Albee using her frame, hook, and woolen materials. My first two rugs had large plain centers and geometrical borders—very uninteresting, for I was copying to a certain degree what Helen Albee was creating from Indian motifs. Everyone thought they were quite wonderful—the first ones made around this area in many years. The colors were harmonious, nothing objectionable, but how I myself disliked them—and from that day I was determined to do something original."

Upon completion of high school, the young artist attended the Rhode Island School of Design, graduating in 1915. Her original intent was to become a landscape painter, but it soon became apparent that her strongest talents were in the field of design. After promising not to converse with the other students, Miss Gammons was admitted to the all-male New Bedford Textile School. She became the first woman graduate, in 1917, taking with her a diploma and the capabilities of a commercial designer. Shortly thereafter, she was hired as chief textile designer for New Bedford's Manville Mills. The position required monthly trips to the company's main office in New York City, excursions she often made in a new Model T Ford. Her career at the mill was short-lived. "This commercialism gave me no satisfaction, just grinding out new patterns every six months, and I left to devote all my time to creating hooked rugs." While pursuing rug hooking interests, Miss Gammons also taught art courses at a local academy, produced and sold artwork, and managed an antique shop on Cape Cod. In 1925, she married Warren Price Tobey, her high school classmate. The couple's first house, in nearby Barrington, Rhode Island, was built from plans drafted by the new bride.

From her Barrington home, Mrs. Tobey began teaching rug hooking classes and producing the countless numbers of hooked rugs that would grace the homes of family and friends and be a source of income needed to help raise the Tobey's three sons.

In 1942, during World War II and after more than thirty years of hooking rugs for sale and pleasure, Mrs. Tobey entered a national needlework competition held in New York City's Madison Square Garden. Her rug, inspired by the family's victory garden, was awarded the grand prize. She also received a week-long invitation to be a guest on the Mary Margaret McBride radio talk show. The popular host was a hooked rug collector and inquired if Mrs. Tobey would make a rug for her. A year later one was designed and crafted to honor McBride's home state of Missouri. The request inspired Mrs. Tobey to create a hooked rug for each of the fifty states. After careful research, she made countless black and white sketches and watercolor patterns before the actual hooking began. The fifty-rug project was started in 1943 and continued through the 1950s and early 1960s. When the state rugs were exhibited at the Providence Art Club, a local Rhode Island television station promised to broadcast a prerecorded interview with Mrs. Tobey. Minutes prior to the show's end, the announcer broke for commercial messages but invited the audience to stay tuned for a segment with Rhode Island's oldest hooker. The eighty-three-year-old rug maker was delighted. Subject of numerous newspaper and magazine articles, the

state rugs were enjoyed by a wide audience, including being exhibited at Bryn Mawr College in Pennsylvania, before becoming part of the permanent collection at the Shelburne Museum in Vermont. The state rug collection and other examples of her handiwork were generously donated to the museum by Mrs. Tobey's three sons, Joel, Joshua, and Jonathan.

The recognition she received on both local and international levels was a source of great pride to Mrs. Tobey and an inspiration to all rug hookers. Tobey rugs were shown at the Rhode Island School of Design and Horticultural Hall in Boston, sent to India as exemplary of American handwork, and chosen to be part of the permanent 20th Century Art Collection of New York City's Metropolitan Museum of Art. Honoring the multi-talented artist, The Providence Art Club sponsored five one-woman shows of her watercolor paintings and hooked rugs.

In later years, Mrs. Tobey was a familiar sight in the Barrington community, pedaling a bicycle about town carrying samples of her latest handiwork. Living independently and in her own home, she continued to paint, hook rugs, and plan for new exhibits until her passing on December 1, 1984, at the age of ninety-one. Throughout her life, Molly Nye Tobey inspired all with her artistic talents, her spirit, and an ability to remain forever young at heart.

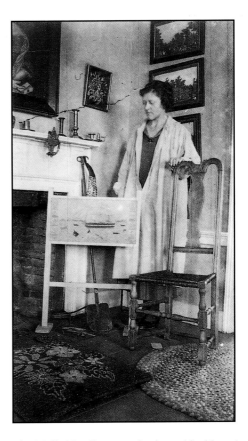

A young Miss Molly Nye Gammons is pictured in this early 1920s photograph with a sampling of the wares she offered for sale at her Cape Cod antique shop in Mattapoisett, Massachusetts. *Courtesy of the Tobey family.*

Surrounded by samples and photographs of her hooked rugs, a newly married Molly Nye Tobey demonstrates her craft. *Courtesy of the Tobey family.*

Draped across her rug hooking frame is one of many room-size rugs designed and hooked by Mrs. Tobey. This photograph was taken in her Barrington, Rhode Island, home during the late 1930s. *Courtesy of the Tobey family..*

Mrs. Molly Nye Tobey, leader of hooked-rug enthusiasts in Barrington, views a design of the Barrington Congregational Church offered at auction this afternoon at the "Hooked-Rug Festival" at the home of Mrs. Foster B. Davis, Rumstick Point, to benefit the restoration fund of the church's steeple, which was swept away in the hurricane, but once again stands in its white stateliness.

A Rhode Island rug hooker comes to the aid of her community church. *Courtesy of the Tobey family.*

Mrs. Tobey hooked this rendering of the Barrington Yacht Club in 1941 as a wedding gift for Mrs. Pete Davis. Note the clever combination of hearts and anchors. Dimensions not available. *Courtesy of the Tobey family.*

Mrs. Tobey won the $100 first prize in hooking and the $300 second grand award with her twelve-foot "Victory Garden" hearth rug. Hooked in 1942, during World War II, this rug paid tribute to all who grew their own produce, contributing to the war effort. Taken from *Woman's Day*, August 1943. *Courtesy of Susan Smidt.*

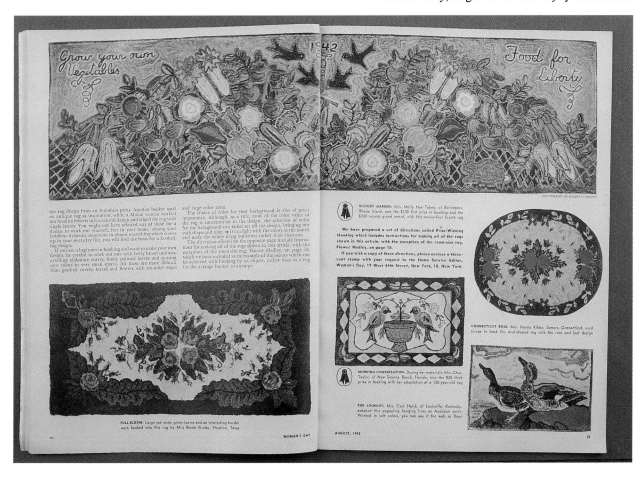

The photographs that follow of the fifty state rugs were reproduced from slides in Mrs. Tobey's personal collection. They were generously shared, along with other photographs and examples of her handiwork, by her three sons, Joel Nye Tobey, Joshua Ashley Tobey and Jonathan Starbuck Tobey.

"Alabama." 39" x 69".

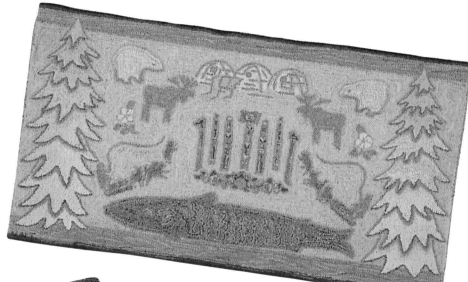

"Alaska." 40" x 75".

"Arizona." 40" x 43".

"Arkansas." 35" x 60".

"California." 40" x 73".

"Colorado." 39" x 56".

"Connecticut." 37" x 60".

"Delaware." 38" x 55".

"Florida." Diameter 44".

"Georgia." 40" x 60".

"Hawaii." 32" x 56".

"Idaho." 40" x 64".

"Illinois." 36" x 59".

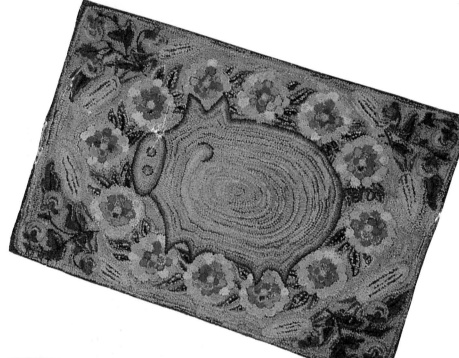

"Indiana." 36" x 53".

"Iowa." 38" x 55".

"Kansas." 35" x 57".

"Kentucky." 30" x 49".

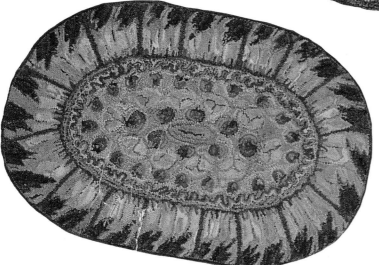

"Louisiana." 36" x 54".

"Maine." 40" x 61".

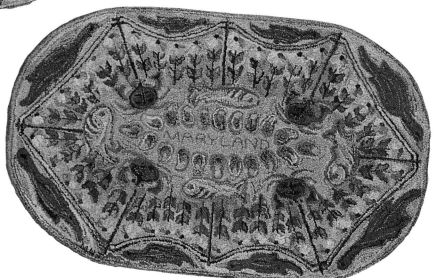

"Maryland." 40" x 66".

"Massachusetts." 40" x 69".

"Michigan." 49" x 66".

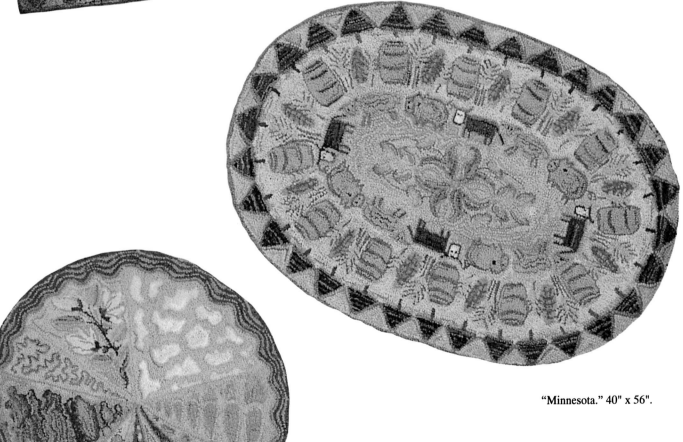

"Minnesota." 40" x 56".

"Mississippi." Diameter 41".

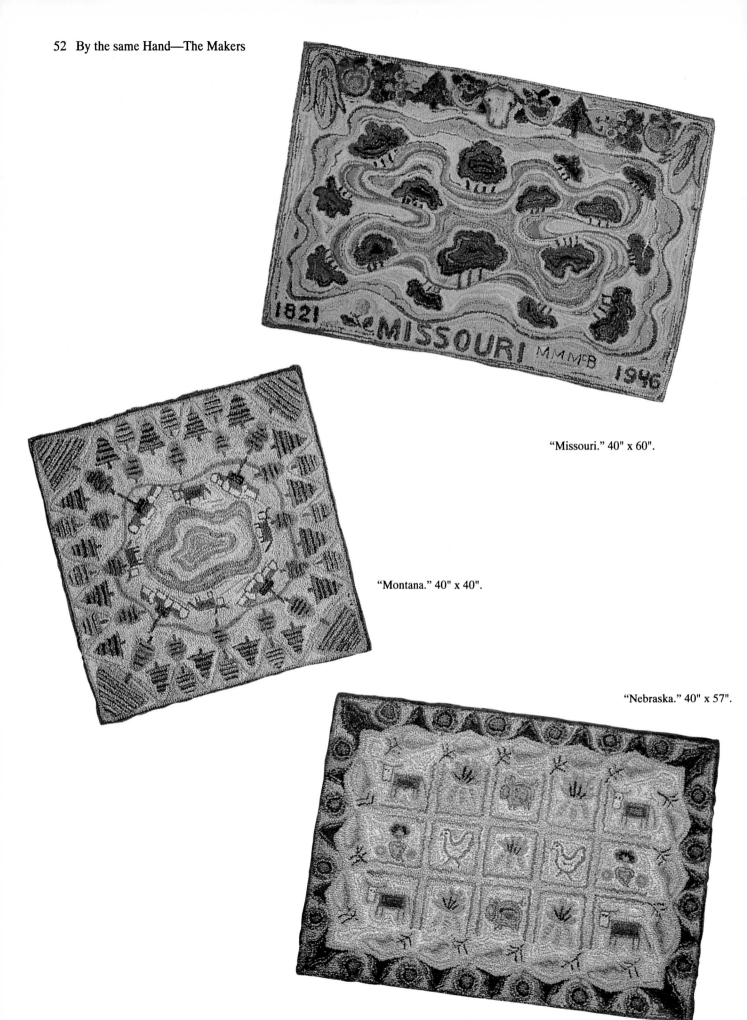

"Missouri." 40" x 60".

"Montana." 40" x 40".

"Nebraska." 40" x 57".

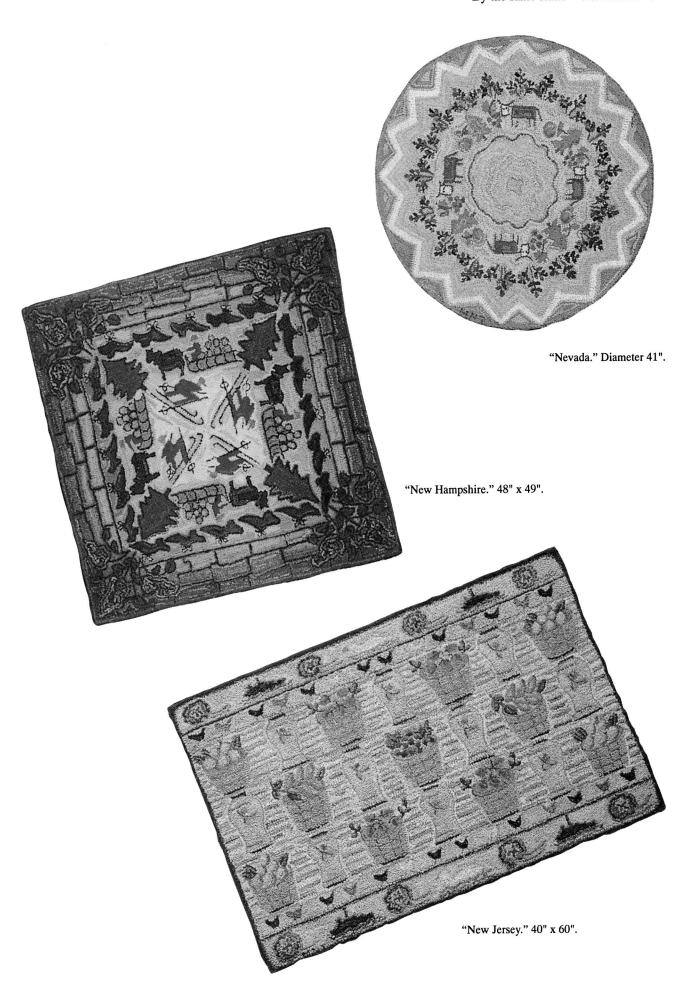

"Nevada." Diameter 41".

"New Hampshire." 48" x 49".

"New Jersey." 40" x 60".

"New Mexico." 36" x 48".

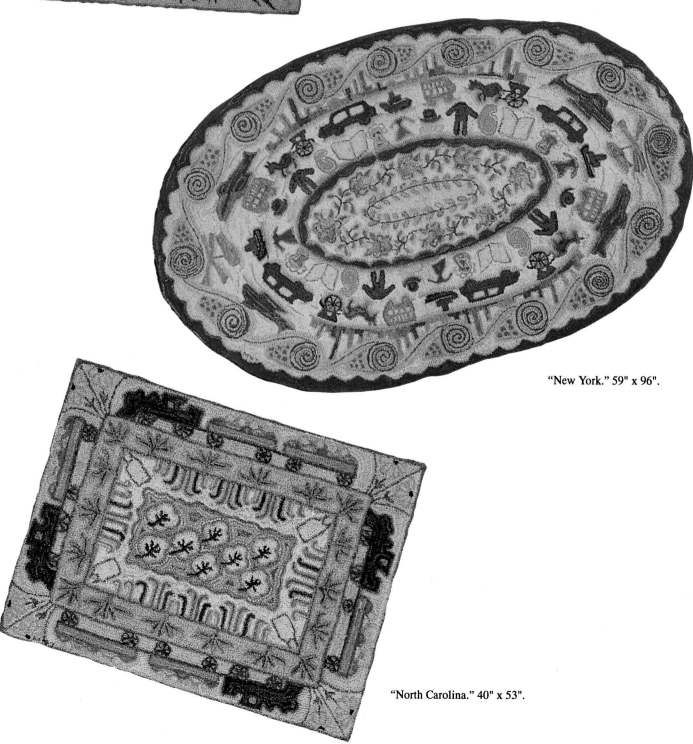

"New York." 59" x 96".

"North Carolina." 40" x 53".

"North Dakota." 40" x 54".

"Ohio." Diameter 48".

"Oklahoma." 32" x 65".

"Oregon." Diameter 40".

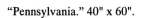

"Pennsylvania." 40" x 60".

"Rhode Island." 33" x 65".

"South Carolina." Diameter 39".

"South Dakota." 39" x 55".

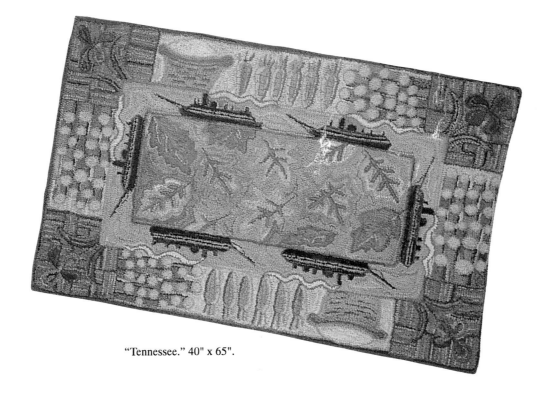

"Tennessee." 40" x 65".

"Texas." 38" x 59".

"Utah." 28" x 43".

"Vermont." 40" x 57".

"Virginia." Diameter 41".

"Washington." Diameter 40".

"West Virginia." Diameter 39".

"Wisconsin." Diameter 48".

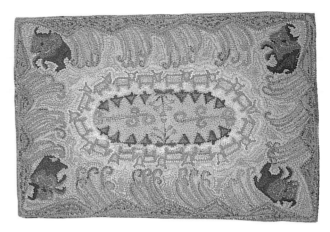

"Wyoming." 32" x 48".

Immersed in her art and surrounded by her work, Mrs. Tobey creates another hooked masterpiece. 1940s. *Courtesy of the Tobey family.*

Mrs. Tobey preferred a rug hook with a bent shank. Pictured is a sampling of some of her favorite tools. *Courtesy of the Tobey family.*

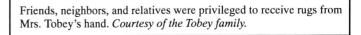

Friends, neighbors, and relatives were privileged to receive rugs from Mrs. Tobey's hand. *Courtesy of the Tobey family.*

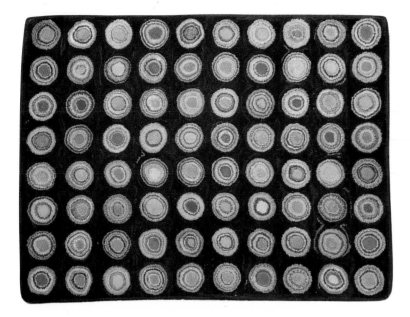

Eighty concentric circles, each with its own personality, fill a navy blue field. 1930-1940. 39" x 53". *Courtesy of Robert and Meredith Gammons.*

A rug of celebration hooked and presented by Mrs. Tobey to commemorate a special wedding day. 1967. 27" x 35". *Courtesy of Donald and Sally (Gammons) Wheeler.*

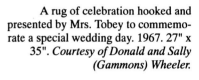

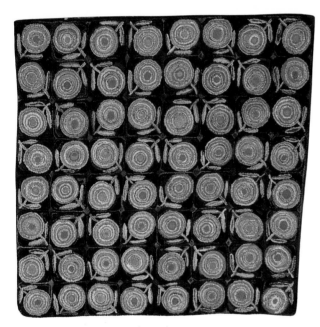

Lollipop flowers by the dozen form a bright and cheerful rug. 1960-1980. 70" x 70". *Courtesy of the Tobey family.*

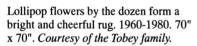

A hooked wedding gift provides a happy welcome to all who visit. 1969. 25" x 40". *Courtesy of Robert and Meredith Gammons.*

"Schooner, Ship, Whale, Brig" sail across a golden sea. 1960-1980.
28" x 63". *Courtesy of the Tobey family.*

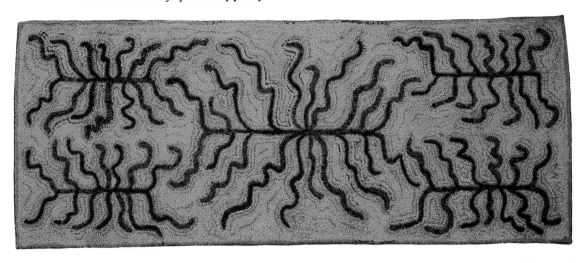

Exploring new textures, mediums, and designs, Mrs. Tobey chose to mix raffia with touches of woolen fabric to complete this unusual and interesting rug. 1960-1980. 29" x 71". *Courtesy of the Tobey family.*

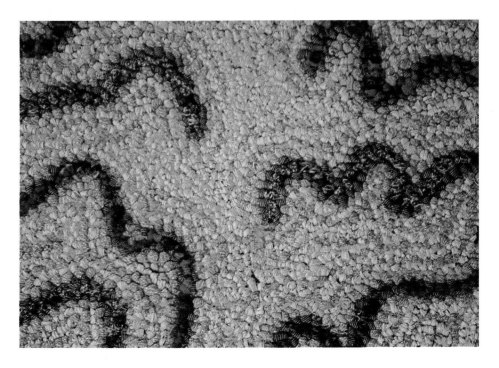

Detail of Mrs. Tobey's raffia and woolen fabric hooked rug.

Accompanied by three of her hooked rugs, a vivacious 75-year-old Mrs. Tobey prepares to pedal her bicycle about town. 1968. *Courtesy of the Tobey family.*

A talented octogenarian reflects on a lifetime of artistic achievement. *Courtesy of the Tobey family.*

George-Edouard Tremblay

My very first recollection of a hooked rug was when I was seven or eight years old. Perched on the edge of our bathtub, I watched as my father submerged in sudsy water a hooked winter scene that for years had hung in my brothers' bedroom. He felt that the wall hanging would benefit from a cleansing. I stared in amazement as streams of color ran from the soaking textile.

Thirty years later, still possessing the ill effects from its time in the tub, the hooked wall hanging was pulled out of the closet and presented to me by my mother. She thought that perhaps I could do something to reclaim its former beauty. The winter scene of a horse-drawn sleigh traveling over a snow-covered lane was purchased in Quebec by my parents during the 1940s for $125. The hooked piece bears the initials G.E.T.

George-Edouard Tremblay was born in 1902 in Baie-Saint-Paul, Quebec. At the age of ten, young Tremblay began to paint. His inspiration came from the fields, flowers, and country folk that were synonymous with the rural landscape of his home. In 1926, he attended l'Ecoles des Artes Domestiques de Quebec. Under the direction of A. O. Beriau, Tremblay was introduced to the art of rug hooking. The scenes he hooked, like those of his paintings, reflected the Quebec countryside.

An exhibit of Tremblay's paintings was held in New York City in 1933. With the success of the show came a suggestion from the Councilor of the Ministry of Commerce to combine his painting and hooking talents. Tremblay began to teach rug hooking in a workshop school in Pointe-au-Pic. The year was 1938. By 1948, the student body numbered three hundred and the school had need of twenty-eight employees. Emile Gaudissard, a renown French tapestry artist, was brought from Paris by the provincial government of Quebec to teach special techniques at Tremblay's school.

The scenic wall hangings created from patterns of Tremblay's paintings and hooked with hand-dyed cotton yarns were sold to tourists and in local art shops. Most carried the initials G.E.T. or G.T., but some were without any signature at all. For forty years, Tremblay and his wife, Marie, maintained the school and workshop. In spite of two fires that forced him to twice rebuild, Tremblay and his staff continued to produce hooked wall tapestries that earned international acclaim. Examples of Tremblay's work were exhibited at the Chateau Frontenac in Quebec, the Royal York Hotel in Toronto, Hotel Reiner Elizabeth in Montreal, British American Oil in Mount-Royal, and the International Museum of Philadelphia. Tremblay closed the school in 1970.

In 1978 Madame Francoise Labbe, a relative of Tremblay's, reopened his studio. The elderly artist would often visit and, with a critical eye, inspect the work being done. Utilizing Tremblay's original sketches, the wall hangings are now made in limited editions and hooked with hand-dyed, color-fast woolen yarns. The colors used are pleasing to the eye and will not fade as the earlier cotton yarns did. Each is signed G.E.T. in the lower right-hand corner. The lower left-hand corner bears the initials of the contemporary hooking artist. Tremblay died on December 30, 1987. He was eighty-five years old. Madame Labbe is the current director of the Art Centre located in Baie-Saint-Paul, Quebec. Hooked tapestries of varying size, including small tabletop mats, wall hangings, and floor rugs, can be purchased in the studio or made to order.

In recent years, Tremblay hooked scenes have attracted the attention of both Canadian and American antique dealers and collectors, though few have been aware of their legacy.

While traveling through Quebec in the 1940s, my parents purchased this hooked Tremblay wall hanging for $125. The artist's initials, G.E.T., though barely visible, appear in the lower right-hand corner of the winter scene. 29" x 37".

A small Tremblay hooked mat of a spring landscape depicts majestic mountains, birch trees, a snow-covered clearing, and the emergence of the season's first green grass. Signed G.E.T. in the lower right-hand corner. 12" x 15". *Courtesy of Anne Boissinot.*

The underside of the spring landscape reveals the mat's true colors. Hand-dyed cotton yarns used during Tremblay's lifetime had a tendency to fade.

Detail of Tremblay's initials, G.E.T., located in the lower right-hand corner of the aforementioned spring landscape.

A summer countryside scene of two men and a horse-drawn cart. The initials G.E.T. appear directly under the horse's hooves. 28" x 35". *Courtesy of Jeremiah Dalton House Antiques.*

George-Edouard Tremblay carefully examines dyed yarns as a rug maker works on the hooked tapestry for British American Oil. Reprinted from *Canadian Crafts in Industry. Courtesy of Shirley Poole.*

British American Oil's Quebec Division office in Mount-Royal commissioned Tremblay to produce a floor-to-ceiling hooked tapestry for their main lobby. The colorful work highlighted profiles of Quebec, as seen on the cover of B-A Oil's *Canadian Crafts in Industry*. It is believed that the pictured booklet was printed and distributed during the mid-1940s. *Courtesy of Shirley Poole.*

A red horse-drawn sleigh, complete with Christmas tree, makes its way through a mountain village. The initials G.E.T., though difficult to see from the topside of the wall hanging, were hooked into the lower right-hand corner. 24" x 30". *Courtesy of Margaret Ruhland.*

Winter's blanket of white covers an isolated country home. A faint G.E.T. is located in the lower right-hand corner. Purchased in Quebec in 1989 for $250. 25" x 32". *Private Collection of Gordon and Susan Scale.*

Evergreen branches ladened with snow partially obscure the view of two woodland cabins. Purchased in Quebec during the 1940s. A barely visible G.T. appears in the lower right-hand corner. 38" x 50". *Private Collection.*

A different interpretation of the two woodland cabins. The initials
G.E.T. were hooked into the lower right-hand corner. 28" x 36".
Courtesy of Margaret Ruhland.

A snowbound chalet is dwarfed by towering trees. Faint initials
appear in the lower right-hand corner. 24" x 30". *Private Collection.*

California Hookin'

From East Coast to West Coast, four generations of Jane Olson's family have enjoyed the tradition of hooking rugs. Jane's mother, Lucy Selen of Worcester, Massachusetts, took rug-making lessons in the 1930s at Rose Cottage, the West Boylston home of renown rug hooking teacher Pearl McGown. As a young girl, Jane would work on her mother's rugs, patiently filling in background area; it was a pastime she did not enjoy. During the early 1940s, Jane began to braid rugs as well as design and hook small pieces. After marriage and a move to California in 1957, the young Mrs. Olson joined a Del Aire area adult education rug hooking group to be among others who shared enthusiasm for her favorite craft. Within two years she was instructing a growing number of students interested in hooking and braiding. Jane earned her teaching credentials from the University of California at Los Angeles and for the next fifteen years conducted adult education classes in quilting and rug hooking.

In addition to giving hooking lessons, Jane designed and sold her own line of preprinted rug patterns. Over the years she purchased the copyrights to patterns belonging to retired rug hooker and businesswoman Mildred Sprout and dye formulas for a popular line of swatches from Clarrise McLain. Communication between her many students and clients across the United States became necessary and for twenty-two years Jane has published a bimonthly instructional newsletter. Her talents as a rug hooking teacher, designer, dye expert, and enthusiastic speaker have made Jane Olson a much-in-demand figure in the rug hooking community. "I love traveling around the country teaching. No matter where my travels take me, I see such wonderful works of art hooked by ruggers," she says.

Currently Jane resides in Inglewood, California, but continues to maintain a busy schedule motoring across the United States spreading the joys of rug hooking. Her sister in Massachusetts, Norma Flodman, also an accomplished hooking artist, helps Jane with the pattern business and often accompanies her on teaching trips. Jane's daughter, Marilyn Orbeck, carries on the family tradition of rug hooking from her home in Santa Barbara, California. From Atlanta, Georgia, Marilyn's daughter and Jane's granddaughter, Kristian Panettiere, is busy bringing rug hooking into the twenty-first century with her "Internet Arts Connection," which features the "Rug Hooker Network." East Coast to West Coast, Jane Olson and family have rug hooking covered.

"Circles" surprises all with a variety of optical illusions. Jane Olson. 1995. 34" x 48". *Courtesy of Jane Olson.*

The "Artemas Scroll" pattern is a copy of an early rug found in the Shrewsbury, Massachusetts, historical home of General Artemas Ward. During the Revolutionary War, Ward was second in command to George Washington. Life-like roses replace the primitive flowers that were in the central motif of the original rug. The scroll design has not been altered. Jane Olson. 1992. 30" x 40". *Courtesy of Jane Olson.*

Using a finely cut strip of woolen fabric (2/32") the hooking artist created "Datura," a detailed study of a flowering member of the nightshade family. Jane Olson. 1996. 20" x 16". *Courtesy of Jane Olson.*

"Kashan Roses," inspired by a Persian design, has a flowering center motif and reversed pattern border. Jane Olson. 1995. 27" x 29". *Courtesy of Jane Olson.*

"Twined Scroll" is a lively pattern whose subtle changes of color were achieved by using dip-dyed woolen materials. Jane Olson. 1996. 34"x 48". *Courtesy of Jane Olson.*

In response to the problems that rug makers often face when hooking foliage, this talented teacher offers "Leaves," a sampler of varied greenery. Jane Olson. 1994. 20" x 30". *Courtesy of Jane Olson.*

Featured on the cover of *Rug Hooking* magazine (July/August 1989) Jane Olson pays homage to "Flying Cloud," a sailing ship of record-breaking speed. Jane Olson. 1987. 24" x 30". *Courtesy of Jane Olson.*

Jule Marie Smith

In the rug hooking world, Jule Marie Smith is known as the woman of a thousand borders. For more than twenty years, the New York hooking artist and teacher has created original-design rugs, framing each with her wide variety of signature edgings. Featured are a sampling of rugs from the artist's hands.

"Bird in Hand" features a pair of black birds sporting bovine crowns. Multicolored hands form the frame. Jule Marie Smith. 1995. 33" x 47". *Courtesy of Jule Marie Smith.*

Birds dart about two horses; one plain and one "A Gentleman's Fancy." Jule Marie Smith. 1993. 41" x 82". *Courtesy of Jule Marie Smith.*

"Flower and Flame" is a hooked interpretation of traditional crewelwork patterns. Jule Marie Smith. 1983. 46" x 70". *Courtesy of Jule Marie Smith.*

"Charlton Idyll" depicts a New York village scene of peace and contentment. A clamshell border complements all. Jule Marie Smith. 1983. 44" x 72". *Courtesy of Jule Marie Smith.*

A Biblical verse is cleverly worked into the scroll-like design that frames this rural home. "Aabo Homestead Rug." Jule Marie Smith. 1985. 36" x 60". *Courtesy of Jule Marie Smith.*

An aerial view of "The Ellm Family Home" is an impressive sight. Geese fly in V formation above a blanket of autumn hued trees. Jule Marie Smith. 1988. 36" x 60". *Courtesy of Jule Marie Smith.*

Pastoral scene of a "Vermont Farm." Jule Marie Smith. 1990. 36" x 60". *Courtesy of Jule Marie Smith.*

Daily activities on an Amish farm are complemented by the patterns of a traditional "Amish Quilt." Jule Marie Smith. 1989. 36" x 60". *Courtesy of Jule Marie Smith.*

"Too Cold To Fish" depicts a frozen wonderland of winter fun. Jule Marie Smith. 1989. 36" x 60". *Courtesy of Jule Marie Smith.*

Days of Victorian Elegance Revisited

In 1907, Prudence Matthews' grandfather, Charles Daniel Riggs, built a cottage along the shore of the St. Lawrence River in Fishers Landing, New York. The picturesque region, known as the Thousand Islands, borders the United States and Canada and was a popular summer resort for wealthy Victorian ladies

A vintage brochure serves as an enticement for the Thousand Islands, a popular vacation resort. *Courtesy of Prudence R. Matthews.*

Rug hooking artist Prudence Matthews poses with a work in progress. *Courtesy of Prudence R. Matthews.*

and gentlemen from both countries. Hotels welcomed guests as early as 1847. A building boom of grand resorts and private estates financed by an assortment of millionaires, including George Pullman of railroad fame, tobacco entrepreneur Charles Emery, Whitman of the candy fortune, and denim king Levi-Strauss, continued until the turn of the century. During the summers of the 1890s, thirteen passenger trains arrived and departed the Thousand Islands area daily. Visitors could stay at a variety of hotels near the train depot or board steamers sailing to one of the many island resorts. The most luxurious accommodations were to be found at the Frontenac Hotel. Built on Round Island in 1881, the hotel had expanded to provide elegant lodging for four hundred guests by 1900. George Pullman urged President and Mrs. Ulysses S. Grant to visit his Thousand Island estate. The four-day presidential stay received national coverage. Soon afterward the elite of New York City and Philadelphia began flocking to the region. In 1882, President Chester A. Arthur made a ten-day visit. The area became one of the most popular seasonal resorts in the United States, attracting a clientele from both the well-to-do and middle classes.

By 1915, the glory days of the Thousand Islands were over. Travel by automobile, concern over World War I, and the fact that several of the grand hotels and estates had been destroyed by fire, combined to bring the resort's era of Victorian elegance to an end.

The Fishers Landing cottage, built by Prudence Matthews' grandfather, remains in her family. Generation after generation have enjoyed boating, swimming, and fishing along the scenic banks of the St. Lawrence River. To chronicle the history of the region and to preserve cherished family memories, Prudence Matthews began in the early 1990s to hook vignettes of another time—the Thousand Islands, 1880-1910.

With the train station featuring George Pullman's private railway car and Charles Emery's Calumet Castle firmly in place, one can see the artist's sketches yet to be hooked. Prudence R. Matthews. 1996. *Courtesy of Prudence R. Matthews.*

The completed "Train Station at Clayton, New York, in the Gay 1900s." Note Round Island's luxurious Frontenac Hotel in the rug's upper right-hand corner. Prudence R. Matthews. 1996. 48" x 72". *Courtesy of Prudence R. Matthews.*

In 1881, the Thousand Islands Steamboat Company, in conjunction with the Folger Company, launched its most famous steamboat, the St. Lawrence. The construction of a massive searchlight mounted on the pilot's cabin made evening tours of the island popular. Prudence R. Matthews. 1995. 34" x 48". *Courtesy of Prudence R. Matthews.*

Detail of the St. Lawrence and its probing searchlight.

George Boldt, a poor German immigrant who made his fortune in the hotel business, purchased Hart Island in the summer of 1893 and renamed it Heart Island. The property was literally reshaped to match its name. The lavish construction of his Rhine River–inspired castle ended abruptly in 1904 with the death of his beloved wife. His $2 million investment was left to the elements. "Boldt Castle" is currently undergoing restoration. Prudence R. Matthews. 1994. 45" x 46". *Courtesy of Prudence R. Matthews.*

"Rock Island Lighthouse," erected in 1847, has guided river-going mariners throughout the years. Prudence R. Matthews. 1993. 39" x 43". *Courtesy of Prudence R. Matthews.*

With his castle abandoned, George Boldt turned his energies to building a yacht house of a grand scale. Prudence R. Matthews. 1995. 48" x 68". *Courtesy of Prudence R. Matthews.*

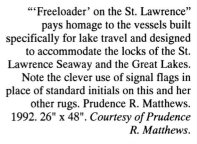

"'Freeloader' on the St. Lawrence" pays homage to the vessels built specifically for lake travel and designed to accommodate the locks of the St. Lawrence Seaway and the Great Lakes. Note the clever use of signal flags in place of standard initials on this and her other rugs. Prudence R. Matthews. 1992. 26" x 48". *Courtesy of Prudence R. Matthews.*

Modern-day view of Rock Island Lighthouse from the artist's Thousand Island cottage. *Courtesy of Prudence R. Matthews.*

Built in 1827, "Tibbitt's Point Lighthouse" was the earliest of seventeen such structures which aided navigation through the challenging waters of the Thousand Islands. It is also the site where the artist's father, Dr. Kenneth Smith, proposed to Ruth, Prudence's mother. Henceforth known as "Engagement Point," the location proved true to its name when son Charles proposed to his future bride, Kristina, there. Prudence R. Matthews. 1994. 23" x 36". *Courtesy of Prudence R. Matthews.*

Each year a variety of meticulously restored antique boats parade in the waterways of the Thousand Islands. "Boat Show." Prudence R. Matthews. 1991. 19" x 51". *Courtesy of Prudence R. Matthews.*

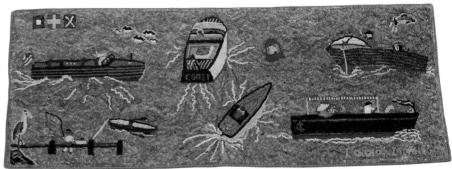

Spiritual Visions

Calling upon her inner spirits, New Hampshire fiber artist Jan Seavey portrays visions with hook and woolen fabrics. "Spirit Journey," "Wolf," and "Inner Remembering" are her trilogy expressing life, balance, and energy.

Detail of "Spirit Journey."

"'Spirit Journey' came to me in a vision. Everything in this wall hanging has a significant meaning to me. It is about life, about balance, and about energy. Ever since I was young, I've had a bond with hawks. It seems that whenever I have to make a decision, large or small, a hawk would appear. It is then that I know that I've made the right choice. A hawk will always be near me in times of struggle and joy. The hawk is located outside the border of the piece because it is free and nothing can confine it. The center represents the balance of energy. Energy flows in an eternal circular pattern. Another representation of balance is the sky blending from night to day." Jan Seavey's "Spirit Journey" was completed in 1994 after five years of work. 42" x 24". *Courtesy of Jan Seavey/ Rising Hawk Studio.*

"Wolf." Jan Seavey. 1996. 14" x 12".
Courtesy of Jan Seavey/Rising Hawk Studio.

"Inner Remembering," a work in progress. Jan Seavey. *Courtesy of Jan Seavey/Rising Hawk Studio.*

Have Hook, Will Travel

Rita O'Neill came to hooking class with the intention of finishing a floral-patterned rug that her mother had started but never finished. She successfully completed the project, but felt a need to create rugs of her own. It wasn't long before the retired teacher from Massachusetts, who paints and loves to travel, recruited her grandson, Jamie O'Neill, to design rugs depicting her favorite places. Pictured are two of Rita's works, the beginning of a series of rugs with travel-related themes.

"Postcards" was designed by Jamie O'Neill and hooked by Rita O'Neill. This underfoot worldwide travel journal recalls favorite places. 1995. 51" x 39". *Courtesy of Rita O'Neill.*

Inspired by a photograph of a scenic California grotto, Rita O'Neill painted a likeness of the location. Pictured is her hooked version of "Grotto." 1996. 34" x 43". *Courtesy of Rita O'Neill.*

Shock Value

Massachusetts fiber artist Susan Smidt continues to shock audiences with hooked images that depart from reality. Her abstracts, in an onslaught of vivid color, provoke interest in all who view her work

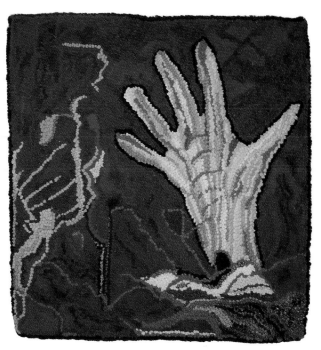

"Hope." Susan Smidt. 1993. 12" x 12". *Courtesy of Susan Smidt.*

"Fyre and Eyece." Susan Smidt. 1992. 21" x 16". *Courtesy of Susan Smidt.*

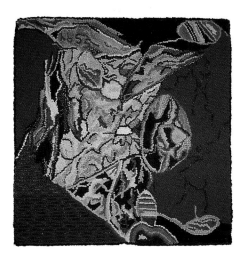

"Clown from Space." Susan Smidt. 1993. 15" x 15". *Courtesy of Susan Smidt.*

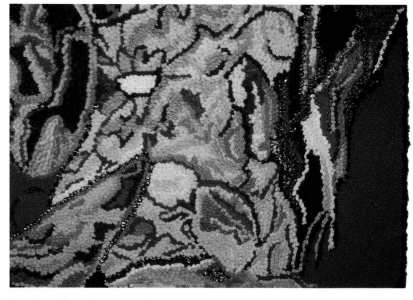

Detail of "Clown from Space."

"Tell Me 'Bout"

With hook in hand, Maryland rug hooking artist Mary Sheppard Burton records the histories of family members. The "Tell Me 'Bout" series was inspired by a bedtime tradition, when all four of her children would gather to hear stories of past generations.

Pictured below and on the following page are snippets from the first seven hooked rugs in Mary Sheppard Burton's "Tell me 'Bout Series." *Courtesy of Mary Sheppard Burton.*

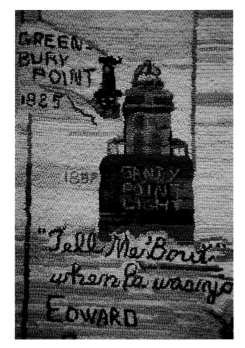

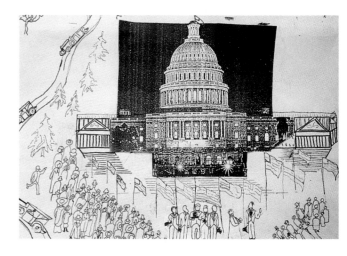

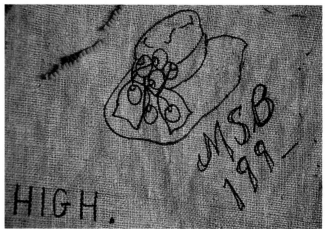

Tennessee Rug Hooker

In one year's time, Elaine Cathcart has produced more rugs than some rug makers hook in a lifetime. Her interest began in 1984 after visiting an exhibit sponsored by the Chattanooga Hookers. Being a wife, mother of two children, and operator of a family owned farm in Athens, Tennessee, forced her to put plans of hooking her own rugs on hold for ten years.

In October 1994, Elaine and a friend began the once-a-week, one-hundred-mile round trip to study with Chattanooga's first lady of rug hooking, Ramona Maddox. Since that time she has been faithfully hooking rugs, using recycled woolen materials and dyeing her fabrics as needed.

A detail of "Elaine" highlights its bold floral design worked in rich, vibrant colors.

Using a combination of as-is and hand-dyed woolen fabrics cut into 1/4"-wide strips, Elaine Cathcart works on "Elaine," a pattern designed for her by Jeanette Szatkowski. *Courtesy of Elaine Cathcart.*

Most rug hookers would require a year or longer to complete an area-size rug, but not Elaine Cathcart. The 5' x 7' floral pattern was started on September 26, 1995, and finished on March 6, 1996. After working a full day on her farm, the prolific rug maker relaxes at night by hooking from 9:30 to 11:30. *Courtesy of Elaine Cathcart.*

"Run Rabbit," the first rug Elaine hooked, combines tweeds, plaids, and solid-colored woolen fabrics. Designed by Patsy Becker. 1994. 25" x 32". *Courtesy of Elaine Cathcart and* Rug Hooking *magazine.*

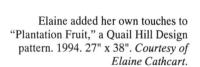

Elaine added her own touches to "Plantation Fruit," a Quail Hill Design pattern. 1994. 27" x 38". *Courtesy of Elaine Cathcart.*

"Lanape" was designed by Patsy Becker and hooked by Elaine Cathcart. Soft tweeds mingle with high-colored woolen fabrics. 1995. 42" x 50". *Courtesy of Elaine Cathcart and* Rug Hooking *magazine.*

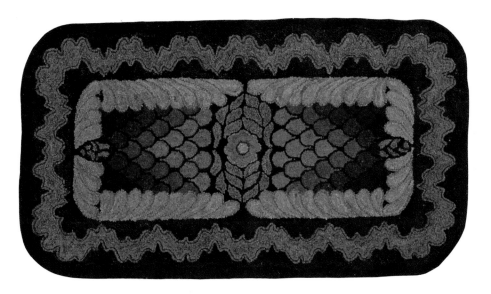

Of the six rugs Elaine Cathcart hooked in twelve months' time, "Norwich" is her favorite. Designed by Lib Callaway. 1995. 30" x 56". *Courtesy of Elaine Cathcart and* Rug Hooking *magazine.*

Elaine adapted "American Country," a Quail Hill Design pattern, to include her favorite animals. 1995. 24" x 65". *Courtesy of Elaine Cathcart and* Rug Hooking *magazine.*

Reminiscent of early yarn-sewn bed rugs, "Bed Rug Fantasy" was designed by Yankee Peddlar and hooked by Elaine Cathcart. 1995. 50" x 40". *Courtesy of Elaine Cathcart and* Rug Hooking *magazine.*

Chéticamp Hooked Rugs

The fishing village of Chéticamp, located in the Cape Breton Island area of Nova Scotia and home to a large Acadian population, is renowned for its finely crafted, hand-hooked rugs.

During the latter half of the 1800s, the French-speaking women of Chéticamp began to hook rugs on potato and bran bags, using the lesser quality wool that came from the legs and bellies of their own sheep. In succeeding years locally spun yarns and those imported from England and Scotland were the choice of the hooking artisans. Potato bags were replaced by commercially made burlap.

By the 1920s, traveling salesmen offering clothing and a variety of household merchandise began knocking at the doors of the Acadian homes, many of which housed beautiful hooked rugs. It wasn't long before shrewd salesmen were bartering for these handmade treasures. Eager to own products that weren't readily available in their rural community, the Acadians quickly parted with their hooked handiwork. Often little was given in exchange for the rugs, which were later taken to the larger urban areas of Canada and the United States and sold for a handsome profit. Although their intentions were not always honorable, these salesmen were responsible for inspiring Chéticamp's most famous cottage industry.

Over the years many others would become involved with Cape Breton's growing and changing hooked-rug trade. Alexander Graham Bell and his wife built a summer home in Nova Scotia, in the countryside of Baddeck. Mrs. Bell, longing for quality handwork, decided to teach the local ladies the art of lace making. During the summer of 1914, Miss Lillian Burke, a New York artist, made a trip to Nova Scotia to visit the Bells. Ten years later, in 1924, Miss Burke would return to Baddeck at the request of Mrs. Fairchild, daughter of the late Mrs. Bell. Mrs. Fairchild hoped to revitalize the lace-making industry her mother had started, with Miss Burke overseeing the project. The lace-making venture failed, but Miss Burke saw the potential market of selling locally made hooked rugs to the growing number of visiting tourists. The Baddeck rug hookers, however, were reluctant to use new designs and more colorful yarns, or to improve their poor technique. Miss Burke and Mrs. Fairchild, looking for other marketable crafts, arrived in Chéticamp in 1927.

There they found talented rug makers who were receptive to the concept of selling their rugs to tourists. Using patterns printed by Miss Burke and the finest of hand-dyed woolen yarns, the Chéticamp hooked rugs took on a new look and attracted buyers. Leaving Mrs. Marie-Jane Doucet, an English-speaking Acadian restaurant owner, to act as her agent, Miss Burke returned to Baddeck, where she and Mrs. Fairchild set up shop and sold rugs that were regularly sent to them from the women, men, and children of Chéticamp, who were now all involved in the business of hooking rugs. The undertaking was monetarily successful. Each winter Miss Burke would travel to New York then return to Cape Breton Island in the summer with orders for hooked rugs, many from an elite clientele requesting custom-made carpets of large dimension.

Eventually Miss Burke opened a gallery and shop in New York. Beginning in a time of economic depression and lasting until World War II, the rug trade not only provided the Acadian families with much-needed income, it was also responsible for making the small fishing village of Chéticamp a landmark and popular tourist attraction. In later years and as more entrepreneurs became involved with the Acadian-made rugs, animosity would arise concerning the division of profits.

Chéticamp hooked rugs came into the hands of many of the world's most rich and famous. Automobile magnate Henry Ford reportedly paid $4,000 dollars for a 114-square-foot hooked map of the world that was placed aboard his yacht. Queen Elizabeth, Prince Charles, and President Dwight Eisenhower, among others, have been recipients of the hooked art. A portrait of Pope John XXIII, work of noted Chéticamp artist Elizabeth Lefort-Hansford, hangs in the Vatican Art Gallery.

Today, many of the rug makers have opened independent shops, offering visitors that come to Chéticamp a sampling of the hooked rugs that have made their Acadian home famous.

Chéticamp hooked mats, old and new, are worked on a burlap base using fine woolen yarns. To the untrained eye they can easily be mistaken for needlepoint tapestries. In recent years, these finely hooked mats have been seen in American antique shops, at antique shows, and for sale at auction. Due to their superb craftsmanship, Chéticamp hooked rugs are often mistaken for Grenfell mats by those who are unaware of their distinctive characteristics and unique heritage.

No travel brochure or postcard from Nova Scotia's Acadian fishing village of Chéticamp would be complete without mention of the area's long and illustrious rug hooking tradition.

A palette of pastel, hand-dyed woolen yarns was used by the Chéticamp rug hookers to create this pleasing-floral design rug. 1950-1970. 25" x 54".

A closer look at the underside of the aforementioned floral rug reveals that the background area was hooked in a pattern of small diamonds, characteristic of many Chéticamp rugs.

"Persian Horse" is a reproduction of a Chéticamp rug bought in 1938 by Lady Tweedsmuir as a Christmas gift for her son and later displayed at Rideau Hall in Ottawa. Lady Tweedsmuir was the wife of Sir John Buchan, First Baron Tweedsmuir (1875-1940), a Scottish author and Governor-General of Canada from 1935 to 1940. 1940-1960. 31" x 44". *Courtesy of Robin Moore Walker.*

Perhaps resulting from a custom order or simply made to attract
American tourists, Acadian rug hookers fashioned nearly identical
twin replicas of this internationally recognized symbol of the United
States Government. 1940-1960. Both measure 33" x 32". *Courtesy of
Russ and Karen Goldberger.*

A detail highlights the fine craftmanship of the eagle and
shield. Note the pattern hooked into the background area.

Hooked by Acadian hands, this rug features an Oriental-style sea serpent. 1940-1960. 33" x 49". *Courtesy of Robin Moore Walker.*

A picture-perfect hooked postcard from the fishing village of Chéticamp, a scenic stop along Nova Scotia's Cabot Trail. 1970-1990. 10" x 12". *Courtesy of Robin Moore Walker.*

While browsing about a yarn shop in Saint Andrews, New Brunswick, during the fall of 1996, I spot this tiny contemporary Chéticamp hooked mat and purchased it for $18.95 Canadian. 5" x 7".

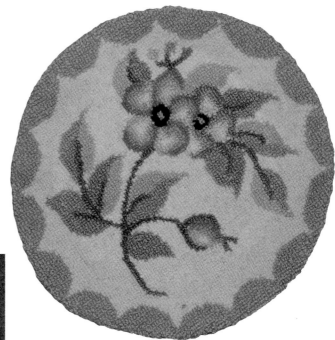

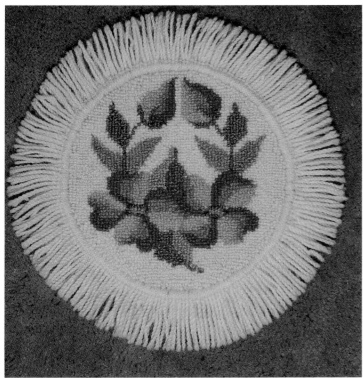

Handicraft shops throughout the Canadian Maritimes offer
Chéticamp hooked rugs and tabletop mats such as these. From top to
bottom: 1980s. Diameter 11". 1960s. Diameter with fringe 10".
1980s. Diameter 10". *Courtesy of Susan Logue.*

3. Collectors—A Passion for Hooked Rugs

William Winthrop Kent

Makers of hooked rugs and hooked rug collectors often find it difficult to locate books devoted to the subject of their enthusiasm. It was even more challenging to find such books during the 1930s and 1940s. Essential in any hooker's or collector's library are W. W. Kent's *The Hooked Rug* (1930), *Rare Hooked Rugs* (1941), and *Hooked Rug Design* (1949). The trilogy was the work of William Winthrop Kent, architect of note and hooked rug connoisseur.

Kent was born of privilege in 1860. The family's prosperity came in part from the Buffalo, New York–based dry goods company Flint and Kent. Young William attended Harvard University in Cambridge, Massachusetts, and graduated among the class of 1882 with a degree in architecture. While pursuing his studies, Kent served as editor of *The Harvard Lampoon.*

Kent earned the reputation of being an architect of merit and was responsible for many outstanding structural designs, including churches, Carnegie libraries, commercial and office buildings, and private residences in the New York area. His work included both interior and exterior design in the United States and abroad. In addition to his architectural skills, Kent was a talented writer. He submitted numerous articles for publication in technical journals and also composed a study of the life of Baldassare Peruzzi, an architect and painter of the fifth century. He married Jessie Adams (of presidential lineage) and was the father of five children. The Kents maintained a New York residence and summered in Orleans, Massachusetts. Their Cape Cod retreat, "Kentucket," encompassed twenty-eight acres along Little Pleasant Bay.

While on a fishing trip in Maine, the state of his birth, William Kent's attention was drawn to the hooked rugs on the floors of the cabin in which he was staying. With this new interest he began to collect and design hooked rugs and eventually authored three books on the subject. *The Hooked Rug*, published in 1930, and *Rare Hooked Rugs*, published in 1941, contain many rugs belonging to "Hooked Rug Magnate" and antique dealer Ralph W. Burnham of Ipswich, Massachusetts. By the 1930s, Burnham was well established as a supplier of both antique hooked rugs and reproductions to an elite clientele. Hooked rugs that came from Burnham's Trading Post graced the floors of the DuPont's Winterthur and the estate of 1920s actor John Mack Brown, as well as being sold in such department stores as Wanamakers, Marshall Fields, and B. Altman & Company. Burnham also helped interior designer Henry Sleeper fill his forty-plus-room

Gloucester, Massachusetts, "cottage" with hooked rugs. It is unclear how the association between William Winthrop Kent and Ralph Burnham began. Perhaps Kent was among the many that sought Burnham out for his selection of choice rugs. Or did Kent have architectural business with Henry Sleeper which then led him to Burnham's door? Regardless of the situation, the association was one of mutual admiration, as is evident in Kent's first two books.

During the 1940s, due to health problems, the Kents moved to La Jolla, California. In the warmer climate, Kent began to hook the rugs he had designed. Drawing upon his architectural background and inspired by world travels, Kent's third book, *Hooked Rug Design*, published in 1949, contains examples of old and new hooked rugs and colored sketches of patterns.

William Winthrop Kent died in 1955. In tribute to his architectural skills, many of the buildings he designed still stand. As we near the twenty-first century, the three Kent hooked rug books are highly regarded and sought after by rug hookers, hooked rug collectors, folk art enthusiasts, and those who treasure hand-crafted textiles.

William Winthrop Kent tends to the shrubbery outside "Kentucket," his summer home on Cape Cod in Orleans, Massachusetts. *Courtesy of Bill Fidalgo.*

"Kentucket," complete with twenty-eight acres along Little Pleasant Bay, was purchased by Kent in 1901. Many of the rugs pictured in this chapter decorated the floors of the Cape Cod retreat. *Courtesy of Bill Fidalgo.*

Plate 9. A primitive, hooked and probably designed by a child in Nova Scotia. Modern and of small size. Gay in coloring. Shows form of Swastika, as revered by North American Indians, I believe, who call it "the four winds."

Reprinted from Page 17 of William Winthrop Kent's *Hooked Rug Design*, published in 1949.

Pictured is a recent photograph of the rug illustrated on Page 17 of Kent's *Hooked Rug Design*. The pattern was hooked on burlap using a variety of materials including cotton jersey and jute twine. From the Kent Collection. 1920-1940. 25" x 34". *Courtesy of Bill Fidalgo.*

Pictured are a selection of hooked rugs photographed at "Kentucket"
in 1941 by Kent's daughter, Charlotte. *Courtesy of Bill Fidalgo.*

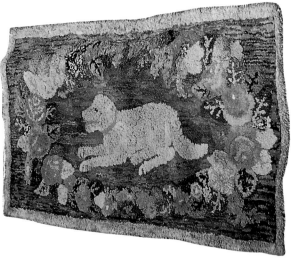

Your attention is drawn to this bold flower-like design flanked by hit-or-miss stripes and diamonds. From the Kent Collection. Early twentieth century. 21" x 38". *Courtesy of Bill Fidalgo.*

An all-over geometric pattern forms an optical illusion of cubes and six-pointed stars. From the Kent Collection. Late nineteenth century. 32" x 62". *Courtesy of Bill Fidalgo.*

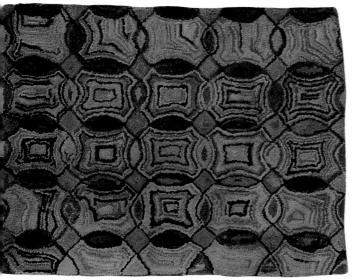

A combination of geometrical shapes attempts to create an optical illusion, but falls short of its goal. Featured on Page 108 of *Rare Hooked Rugs*, Kent makes note that this rug is of Canadian origins. From the Kent Collection. Late nineteenth century. 39" x 51". *Courtesy of Bill Fidalgo.*

Haphazard multicolored lines surround a block motif composed of conjoined pairs of spades. From the Kent Collection. Early twentieth century. 40" x 51". *Courtesy of Bill Fidalgo.*

Detail of the spade motif and background.

A monogrammed diamond is framed by an unusual combination of roses and ears of corn. From the Kent Collection. Late nineteenth century. 31" x 52". *Courtesy of Bill Fidalgo.*

Large spade-shaped leaves and crude scrolls overpower a small central cluster of childlike flowers. From the Kent Collection. Late nineteenth century. 35" x 51". *Courtesy of Bill Fidalgo.*

A serrated border surrounds simple floral sprays. From the Kent Collection. Early twentieth century. 20" x 36". *Courtesy of Bill Fidalgo.*

COLLECTION OF MRS. A. B. SMITH, LA JOLLA, CALIF.

Plate 158. Primitive from Northern Ohio. Lion and Palms design from E. Ross & Co.'s book No. 7. Often used, origin unknown. Also used by E. S. Frost. (See Chapter X)

Reprinted from Page 128 of William Winthrop Kent's *Rare Hooked Rugs*, published in 1941.

The "Lion and the Palms" hooked rug that was pictured in Kent's *Rare Hooked Rugs* and ascribed in 1941 to Mrs. A. B. Smith of La Jolla, California, eventually made its way to the East Coast. The popular pattern of a reclining lion was found among the collection of hooked rugs at "Kentucket." From the Kent Collection. Late nineteenth century. 34" x 73". *Courtesy of Mariah Calhoun Fidalgo.*

Multicolored fronds frame a stylized floral arrangement. From the Kent Collection. Early twentieth century. 38" x 39". *Courtesy of Bill Fidalgo.*

A traditional bouquet of cabbage roses is complemented by the mirror image pattern of twin cornucopias overflowing with delicate blooms. From the Kent Collection. Late nineteenth century. 28" x 48". *Courtesy of Bill Fidalgo.*

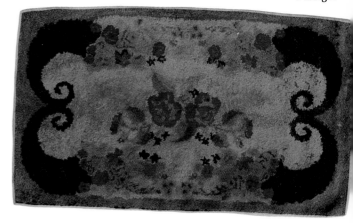

Two clusters of roses, buds, and greenery rest atop a varigated brown field. From the Kent collection. Early twentieth century. 34" x 74". *Courtesy of Bill Fidal*go.

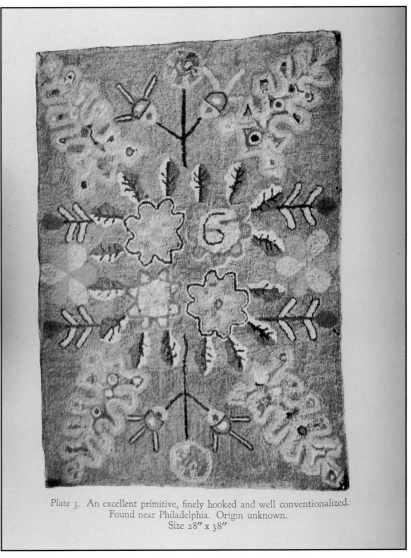

Plate 3. An excellent primitive, finely hooked and well conventionalized. Found near Philadelphia. Origin unknown. Size 28" x 38"

Bold C-shaped scrolls join with decorative floral accents to make a pleasing runner. From the Kent Collection. Early twentieth century. 34" x 79". *Courtesy of Bill Fidalgo.*

Reprinted from Page 2 of William Winthrop Kent's *Rare Hooked Rugs*, published in 1941.

Keeping in mind that color reproduction in the 1930s and early 1940s was not always true, it is difficult to determine if the rug pictured is the same rug that appeared on Page 2 of Kent's *Rare Hooked Rugs*. It is the opinion of this author that perhaps Kent himself or a commissioned rug maker hooked a likeness of the rug he deemed worthy of one of the book's few color plates. Close examination of the photo and the actual rug reveals some variations of small details. From the Kent Collection. Early twentieth century. 28" x 39". *Courtesy of Bill Fidalgo.*

Reprinted from Page 159 of William Winthrop Kent's *Hooked Rug Design*, published in 1949.

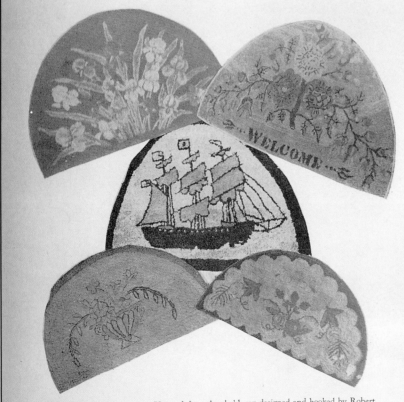

Plate 124. Welcome rugs. *Upper left,* a threshold rug designed and hooked by Robert N. and H. Daniel, Los Angeles, California. Excellent in design and execution. *Upper right,* from collection of Mrs. E. C. Gude, Mill Farm, White Plains, New York. Origin unknown. (Photo by C. A. Kent.) *Center,* a primitive, from the collection of Mrs. E. C. Gude. (Photo by C. A. Kent.) *Lower left,* a primitive, done in pastel; white field. Delicate and graceful composition. (Photo by C. A. Kent.) *Lower right,* maker unknown. Colorful flowers and green leaves on gray field. W. W. Kent collection. (Photo by C. A. Kent.)

[159]

It is believed that this Persian-inspired pattern was designed and hooked by Kent. In efforts to mimic its knotted counterpart, a decorative fringe was added. From the Kent Collection. 1920-1940. 23" x 44". *Courtesy of Bill Fidalgo.*

The once "white field," as described by Kent on Page 159 in *Hooked Rug Design,* of this welcome mat of "delicate and graceful composition" has turned gray with age. From the Kent Collection. 1920-1940. 20" x 35". *Courtesy of Bill Fidalgo.*

After a move to La Jolla, California, in the early 1940s, Kent was able to hook some of the patterns he had designed. Conventional flowers, scrollwork, and most of the outer border of this rug were fashioned from strips of varied cotton fabrics. The background was hooked of jute twine, a method popular with many Canadian rug makers of that era. From the Kent Collection. 1942. 27" x 44". *Courtesy of Bill Fidalgo.*

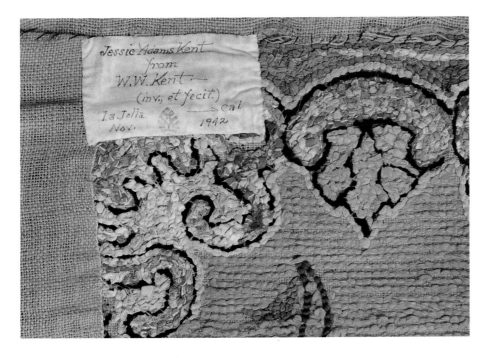

Kent attached a cotton label to the underside of the aforementioned rug. From his documentation we learn that this rug was a gift for his wife, Jessie Adams Kent. Translated from the Latin "inv., et fecit" means "he invented, he made." Hooked in La Jolla, California, the rug was either presented or completed in November 1942. Kent's stamped hallmark appears in the middle of the label's lower edge.

This hooked imitation of an Oriental rug combines a variety of geometrical shapes. From the Kent Collection. 1920-1940. 31" x 46". *Courtesy of Bill Fidalgo.*

"Changsha" was designed and hooked by Kent in 1943. The intricate central motif and outer frame were created from a variety of cotton fabrics. Jute twine was used for the background field. From the Kent Collection. 1943. 27" x 38". *Courtesy of Bill Fidalgo.*

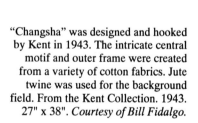

According to the label attached to the underside of "Changsha," Kent's rug, hooked in 1943, was made in tribute to the city of that name, where, in 1941, the Chinese defeated the Japanese.

Bertram K. and Nina Fletcher Little

One of the great collections of American folk art was assembled by Bertram K. and Nina Fletcher Little. The young married couple, living in a modest Cambridge, Massachusetts, apartment, began acquiring antiques during the mid-1920s. The purchase of an 1825 weekend cottage with no modern conveniences about thirty-five miles west of Boston in Hudson, Massachusetts, brought about the need for additional furnishings. Initially believing that antiques would not fit in their budget, the Littles, upon the encouragement of Bertram's cousin, Edna (later Mrs. Arthur Greenwood, who gave and willed her collection to the Smithsonian and Sturbridge Village), sought out New England furniture and related decorative art. By frequenting country auctions, antique shows and shops, and buying directly from estates, the Littles accumulated a grand array of historically interesting objects. As their eclectic collection grew, the family expanded to include three children, and a move to larger accommodations became necessary. Year after year the search for and acquisition of Americana continued.

The Littles maintained two historic homes until they both died in their nineties. Winters were spent at the Federal style 1810 Pumpkin House in Brookline, Massachusetts, and summers at the one-hundred-and-sixty-five acre Cogswell's Grant in the north shore community of Essex. Each home was filled with antique treasures, all carefully researched and documented, but used daily by family members.

During the course of more than six decades of collecting, Nina Little wrote numerous articles for the antique trade papers and magazines, authored several books, lectured, cataloged, and curated museum exhibits of American art in New England, New York City, and Williamsburg, Virginia. Bertram Little's affiliation with the Society for the Preservation of New England Antiquities began in 1928 as recording secretary. From 1947 until his 1970 retirement, he was director of the Society. Bertram was also a member of the Walpole Society. Jointly the Littles were recipients of several prestigious awards for their scholarly contributions to the study of early Americana.

Cogswell's Grant, named for John Cogswell, to whom the land was granted in 1636, was purchased by the Littles in the late 1930s. The homestead, built between 1730 and 1740, and its remarkable contents and expansive agricultural fields were given to the Society for the Preservation of New England Antiquities by the Littles in the early 1990s. At the time of this writing, Cogswell's Grant is undergoing restoration. The property is scheduled to open to the public in the spring of 1998.

The Littles acquired a few hooked rugs in the 1920s for use in their country retreat. Not until the early 1950s did they seriously begin to collect a variety of floor coverings which included yarn-sewn, shirred, and hooked rugs.

Cogswell's Grant, in Essex, Massachusetts, was the summer home of noted antiquarians Bertram K. and Nina Fletcher Little. The circa 1730 homestead, its remarkable contents, and surrounding agricultural fields were given to the Society for the Preservation of New England Antiquities by the Littles in the early 1990s. Currently undergoing restoration, Cogswell's Grant is scheduled to open to the public in the spring of 1998. *Courtesy of the Society for the Preservation of New England Antiquities.*

A sizeable, full-colored hooked rug of abstract floral pattern brightens the floor of the guest chamber at Cogswell's Grant. Varieties of delicate foliage and flowers randomly encircle bold, rose-like blossoms. Working on a burlap base, the early rug maker hooked with a varied assortment of materials including woolen fabrics, cottons, and yarns. 1860-1880. 9' x 9'. *Courtesy of the Society for the Preservation of New England Antiquities.*

Placed beside its large and lively neighbor is a small hooked mat of uncomplicated design. Possibly of Canadian origins. Early twentieth century. *Courtesy of the Society for the Preservation of New England Antiquities.*

A detail of the aforementioned hooked rug highlights a section of the abstract floral pattern and its ever-changing background.

Another detail reveals bunches of grapes intermingled with blooms, buds, and greenery.

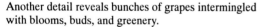

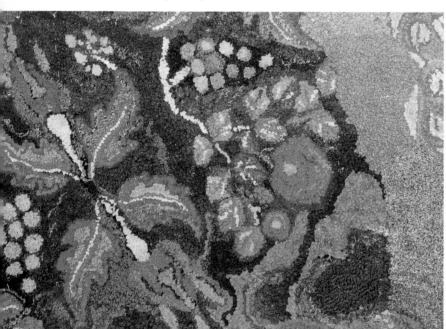

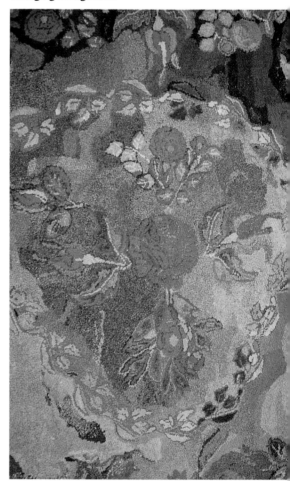

The southwest chamber as it appeared when the Littles were in residence. From the article entitled "Antiques in Domestic Settings" in *Antiques* magazine, June 1940. Photography by T. F. Hartley. *Courtesy of the Society for the Preservation of New England Antiquities.*

A traditional rose and scroll pattern hooked rug rests beside the southwest chamber door, just as it did more than fifty years ago in the aforementioned 1940 photograph. Early twentieth century. *Courtesy of the Society for the Preservation of New England Antiquities.*

In the early 1950s, the Littles began to seriously collect a variety of floor coverings which included yarn-sewn, shirred, and hooked rugs. The handsome rug of curving vines in the foreground was crafted by the technique of pleated shirring. In a tedious and repetitive process, strips of tightly woven wool were folded and stitched to a fabric foundation. 1830-1850. To the left of the shirred rug is a partial view of a popular hooked geometric pattern. Early twentieth century. Placed by the southwest chamber door is the hooked rug of traditional rose and scroll pattern that was pictured in the June 1940 issue of *Antiques* magazine. Early twentieth century. *Courtesy of the Society for the Preservation of New England Antiquities.*

A diminutive mat of raised floral design adorns this bureau in the southwest chamber. Hooked on linen. Four rows of braiding decorate and protect delicate perimeters. 1870-1890. *Courtesy of the Society for the Preservation of New England Antiquities.*

In this rug of muted tones, simplified scrolls frame a mixed bouquet. Southwest chamber. 1890-1910. *Courtesy of the Society for the Preservation of New England Antiquities.*

Ready to warm the feet and brighten the day, a popular Frost "Turkish" pattern hooked rug awaits bedside. 1890-1910. *Courtesy of the Society for the Preservation of New England Antiquities.*

Ragged and torn hooked rugs were often cut down and fashioned into smaller rugs. Such was the history of this bureau-top mat of clamshell design. Early twentieth century. *Courtesy of the Society for the Preservation of New England Antiquities.*

Left: The bold design of this early yarn-sewn coverlet dominates the first-floor guest chamber. A more subdued hooked rug of the double wedding ring quilt pattern rests alongside. 1880-1900. *Courtesy of the Society of the Preservation of New England Antiquities.*

The June 1940 issue of *Antiques* magazine featured an article entitled "Antiques in Domestic Settings." Pictured is the "Guest Room" of Cogswell's Grant complete with hooked rugs. Photography by T. F. Hartley. *Courtesy of the Society for the Preservation of New England Antiquities.*

A hooked mat of squares and triangles decorates a round bedside table. Early twentieth century. *Courtesy of the Society for the Preservation of New England Antiquities.*

Barbara Johnson

Barbara Johnson's collection of hooked rugs is the envy of any rug fancier. The expansive array includes rugs of geometric, abstract, and floral motif, as well as beasts, birds, and pictorials. The collector's personal preference is for rugs of abstract design. Says Ms. Johnson, "I love all my rugs, but delight in the wild and imaginative ones."

At a Sotheby's auction preview, her attention was drawn to a small cotton and wool rag rug hooked about 1900. The 24- by 19-inch example of textile folk art depicted a primitive image of a man in a sheep-driven cart. When the rug went up for auction, the winning bid belonged to Barbara Johnson. Much to her surprise, the sale also included eight other hooked rugs that had not been listed in the catalog. Each of the rugs was quite different from the one that had sparked her interest. The nine rugs were the beginning of a growing collection.

The Squibb Gallery of Princeton, New Jersey, presented an exhibit and catalog of a select fifty-six hooked rugs from the Johnson collection during December 1988 and January 1989. These pages highlight several of the rugs that were on display there, with others from her collection.

Barbara Johnson's hooked rugs have been shared with the public in museums, galleries, and publications. As the most serious of collectors often do, she refines her collection from time to time by acquiring choice rugs and parting with others. When a Barbara Johnson hooked rug goes up for auction, the trade papers are sure to make note of its special owner, and the auctioneer can be assured of a large and attentive bidding audience.

"Mennonite Sun" is a bold design executed in bright colors, resulting in a dynamic display. Made in Pennsylvania. 1920-1940. 6'1" x 8'10".
Courtesy of the Barbara Johnson Collection.

Quilt patterns also make attractive hooked rug patterns. "Log Cabin." Made on Nantucket Island, Massachusetts. 1870-1890. 34" x 49". *Courtesy of the Barbara Johnson Collection.*

The geometric pattern sometimes referred to as "Tumbling Blocks" is popular with rug hookers as well as quilters. Made in Pennsylvania. 1870-1890. 76" x 20". *Courtesy of the Barbara Johnson Collection.*

A repeat composition of "Clouds" travels across bands of changing colors. Purchased in New York. 1870-1890. 33" x 61". *Courtesy of the Barbara Johnson Collection.*

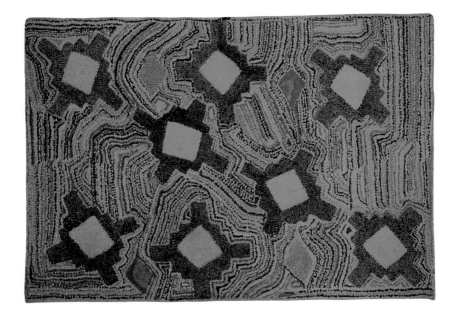

"Olive Asteroids" bounce about a striated field. 1870-1890. 34" x 50". *Courtesy of the Barbara Johnson Collection.*

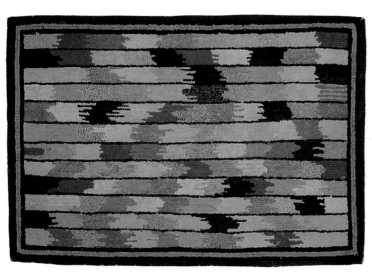

Jagged bits of color are neatly contained. "Intertwined." 1910-1930. 30" x 43". *Courtesy of the Barbara Johnson Collection.*

"Adorsed." [sic] The maker of this hooked rug was obviously influenced by the totem poles carved and painted by Indian tribes of the northwest coast of North America. Erected before their houses, totem poles were symbolic of family lineage and mythical and historical incidents. Purchased in New York. 1890-1910. 36" x 44". *Courtesy of the Barbara Johnson Collection.*

Made in Lancaster County, Pennsylvania, "Greek Flower Pot" is reminiscent of Pennslyvania Dutch folk art with an added European flair. 1890-1910. Diameter 32". *Courtesy of the Barbara Johnson Collection.*

"Kin" is a truthful but not competent speller's commentary on her husband's relatives. Designed by James L. and Mercedes Hutchinson of Brooklyn, New York. Mr. Hutchinson owned a circus and it is believed that he had circus performers hook his rugs. Found in Pennsylvania. 1910-1930. 32" x 53". *Courtesy of the Barbara Johnson Collection.*

A hooked tribute to our nation's father, "General Washington." Found in Richmond, Virginia. 1880-1900. 29" x 53". *Courtesy of the Barbara Johnson Collection.*

Flanked by preening "Mermaids," a poetic verse praises the lovely ladies of the deep, yet cautions those who might encounter them. 1920-1930. 36" x 55". *Courtesy of the Barbara Johnson Collection.*

"M.A.D. Cats." Two nearly identical cats pose on a patchwork floor. Multicolored striations form a lively frame around the pair. Made in Rhode Island. 1875-1895. 26" x 45". *Courtesy of the Barbara Johnson Collection.*

"Roy." This contemporary, childlike hooked portrait of a favorite pig was sewn into the center of an older braided rug. Found in New Hampshire. Composed in 1970. Diameter 40". *Courtesy of the Barbara Johnson Collection.*

With alert, glowing eyes, "Smut" the cat watches all. Hooked by Ethel Bishop. Mid twentieth century. 33" x 17". *Courtesy of the Barbara Johnson Collection.*

Anna B. McCoy

Painter Anna B. McCoy covers the floors of her Pennsylvania home with mid to late nineteenth and early twentieth century hooked rugs. Her rug gallery, which she describes as "little paintings on the floor," has been growing for more than thirty years.

As a young child, Anna B. accompanied her parents and siblings on antique hunts in Maine. She recalls visiting one antique dealer in particular, a gentleman from the coastal town of Rockland, whose shop was filled with a variety of treasures including stacks and stacks of old hooked rugs. Pleasurable hours were spent viewing each rug, carefully inspecting and selecting. The experience left a lasting impression on the young collector-to-be.

Blocks tumble around three central, six-pointed stars. Amoeba-like shapes grace each end of this playful hooked runner. Late nineteenth century. 19" x 58". *Courtesy of Anna B. McCoy.*

A diamond and circle chain forms a ring around five posies. 1910-1930. 24" x 58". *Courtesy of Anna B. McCoy.*

A vibrant, oversized leaf sits at each corner framing a diamond-shaped field of cabbage roses, abundant buds, and greenery. Early twentieth century. 24" x 60". *Courtesy of Ann B. McCoy.*

Diamonds within a diamond are enhanced by a subdued swirling background. Late nineteenth century. 32" x 57". *Courtesy of Anna B. McCoy.*

Alternating scalloped chevrons and intertwined ovals race uninterrupted across this lively rug. Early twentieth century. 54" x 106". *Courtesy of Anna B. McCoy.*

Possibly a sister to the aforementioned "diamonds within a diamond." In this rug, diamonds give way to stars. Both share a subdued swirling background. Late nineteenth century. 38" x 44". *Courtesy of Anna B. McCoy.*

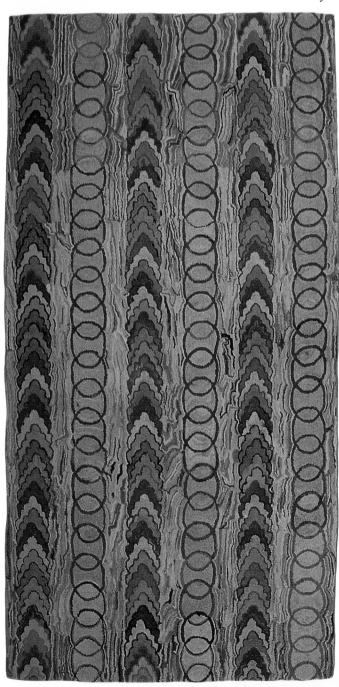

Simple flowers add whimsy to a traditional Oriental rug pattern. 1920-1940. 44" x 63". *Courtesy of Anna B. McCoy.*

Early floral cluster within a fine tray-like enclosure is surrounded by large stemmed blossoms and foliage. A wavy scalloped ribbon borders all. Mid to late nineteenth century. 40" x 80". *Courtesy of Anna B. McCoy.*

A trio of medallions dominate a mosiac field. Early twentieth century. 35" x 78". *Courtesy of Anna B. McCoy.*

A simple, cloud-like shape plays host to a multicolored star. The star motif is repeated in each corner. 1910-1930. 37" x 54". Courtesy of Anna B. McCoy.

Multicolored hit-or-miss quadrants are reminiscent of a window and sash. Early to mid twentieth century. 34" x 41". *Courtesy of Anna B. McCoy.*

An eye-catching, possibly southwestern-inspired theme is contained by ornamental fan motifs. Late nineteenth to early twentieth century. 35" x 69". *Courtesy of Anna B. McCoy.*

A creative rug maker took artistic license with this Edward Sands Frost pattern of a reclining lamb. Early twentieth century. 29" x 45". *Courtesy of Anna B. McCoy.*

This rug's large central shield commands attention. Mid twentieth century. 34" x 42". *Courtesy of Anna B. McCoy.*

An interpretation of a familiar old pattern of crossed sticks and roses. 1910-1930. 32" x 54". *Courtesy of Anna B. McCoy.*

A lineup of autmun leaves, each
slightly different. Early to mid
twentieth century. 35" x 37". *Courtesy
of Anna B. McCoy.*

This hooked rug's background of
medallion-like tiles is accented by a
grid of large crosses. Late nineteenth to
early twentieth century. 33" x 43".
Courtesy of Anna B. McCoy.

A graphic compilation of geometric
forms is softened by an array of
flowers. Early to mid twentieth century.
28" x 43". *Courtesy of Anna B. McCoy.*

Rosettes in triplicate decorate this small
hooked mat. 1920-1940. 16" x 37".
Courtesy of Anna B. McCoy.

Jamie Wyeth

The appeal of folk art hooked rugs does not go unnoticed
by artist Jamie Wyeth.

A two-star rooster is flanked by his subordinates. Early twentieth
century. 38" x 79". *Courtesy of Jamie Wyeth.*

Two black crows investigate a lush bouquet. Mid twentieth century.
23" x 37". *Courtesy of Jamie Wyeth.*

Quiet Collectors

And then there are quiet collectors who appreciate hooked rugs and are willing to share them for all to enjoy.

Silent and serene, a gray dove perches on a delicate branch. Early twentieth century. 45" x 37". *Private Collection.*

Varieties of delicate vegetation emerge from two outspreading and imposing leaves. 1910-1930. 30" x 58". *Private Collection.*

A diminutive bunny sits contentedly amid a riot of brilliant shapes and stylized flowers. Late nineteenth to early twentieth century. 34" x 60". *Private Collection.*

Bold, crenulated borders secure a floral oval. 1890-1910. 26" x 43". *Private Collection.*

A couchant lion holds court on this popular patterned piece. Early twentieth century. 32" x 57". *Private Collection.*

A lone deer ventures from the woodlands to an open meadow. 1920-1940. 30" x 48". *Private Collection.*

Muted colors predominate in this classic floral-patterned rug. 1920-1940. 35" x 57". *Private Collection.*

Robin Moore Walker

Canadian collector Robin Moore Walker first took notice of Grenfell art while browsing about an Ontario antique show during the late 1970s. She was intrigued by the northern themes that the Newfoundland and Labrador hooked mats, made during the first forty years of the twentieth century, depicted. Polar bears, icebergs, and dog teams portrayed in subtle, time-faded colors appealed to her artistic eye. The finely hooked textiles displayed a craftsmanship rarely seen, that of an era long past.

With spirited determination, Robin frequented antique shows and shops and attended countless auctions, purchasing only the most exemplary of Grenfell mats. Contacts were made and relationships were formed with the very small number of dealers in Canada, the United States, and England that specialize in Grenfell items.

Today, almost twenty years later, Robin's collection is extensive and impressive and has grown to include books, carvings, and other handmade trinkets sold to support the medical and educational work of Dr. Wilfred T. Grenfell.

Many of her Grenfell mats are reminiscent of landscape paintings. Mat makers painstakingly hooked tiny loops of silk and rayon in an attempt to mimic the perspective and natural shading of the northern topography. But Robin's favorites are those mats that are just a wee bit off. Perhaps they were hooked by a novice or worked by an elder Labradorian whose eyesight failed in the dim glow of a kerosene lamp. Sled dogs resemble poodles, flying birds are obese, and falling snow is represented by oversized brown polka dots. These mats are folksy and fun. And cherished by Robin Moore Walker, who calls them "wonky" and "wonderful."

The North Wind blows down upon Newfoundland and Labrador. Silk and rayon on burlap. Early twentieth century. 28" x 19". *Courtesy of Robin Moore Walker.*

Close attention was paid to the details of perspective and shadowing in this Northern scene of dog team, komatik, and drivers. Artist Steve Hamilton was responsible for the design. Cotton, silk, and rayon on burlap. Early twentieth century. 34" x 46". *Courtesy of Robin Moore Walker.*

The Northern Lights form a backdrop for a dog team and drivers.
Uncommon for this pattern is the partial depiction of the lead dog and
additional dog trailing behind the komatik. Brin (jute) on burlap with
the exception of a silk and rayon sky. Early twentieth century. 15" x
50". *Courtesy of Robin Moore Walker.*

Dog teams and drivers were a popular
theme for Grenfell hooked mats.
Human faces were almost always
hidden by hoods or left blank, with no
indication of any facial features. These
hardy Northern men atypically possess
eyes, noses, and mouths. Silk and rayon
on burlap with brin (jute) dogs. Early
twentieth century. 27" x 39". *Courtesy
of Robin Moore Walker.*

Though reportedly no young children
were known to have hooked mats for
the Grenfell Labrador Industries, this
whimsical depiction of the popular dog
team and driver pattern most certainly
has childlike qualities. Cotton on
burlap. Early twentieth century. 27" x
33". *Courtesy of Robin Moore Walker.*

In place of a dog team, this sturdy caribou pulls a komatik of Red Cross supplies. Cotton on burlap. Early twentieth century. 27" x 38". *Courtesy of Robin Moore Walker.*

An Inuit figure watches a distant dog team as Northern Lights dance above the horizon. Silk and rayon on burlap. Early twentieth century. 27" x 20". *Courtesy of Robin Moore Walker.*

As a bird flies overhead, a faithfully rendered polar bear gazes into icy waters. Silk, rayon, and cotton on burlap. Early twentieth century. 40" x 26". *Courtesy of Robin Moore Walker.*

A hooked panel of dog team and driver decorates this bag made for holding knitting needles. Silk and rayon on burlap. 1940-1960. 5" x 14" x 4". *Courtesy of Robin Moore Walker.*

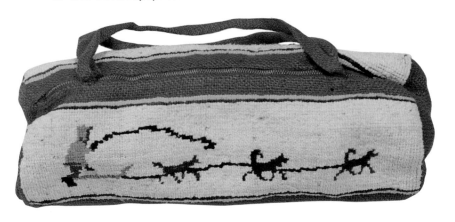

Two rather thin polar bears are pictured on separate ice floes. An iceberg of odd configuration floats in the background sea. Cotton on burlap with polar bears hooked of woolen yarns. Early twentieth century. 19" x 31". *Courtesy of Robin Moore Walker.*

A fuzzy polar bear pauses and sniffs the frigid air. Silk and rayon on burlap with attached seal fur. 1940-1960. 12" x 13". *Courtesy of Robin Moore Walker.*

A simple study of the Northern puffin. Silk, rayon, and cotton on burlap. Early twentieth century. 11" x 9". *Courtesy of Robin Moore Walker.*

Yellow ducks of graduating size march across a sea of blue. Cotton on burlap. Early twentieth century. 17" x 27". *Courtesy of Robin Moore Walker.*

Perched on a patchwork cliff, this puffin sports a distinctive red, white, and blue striped beak. Silk, rayon, and cotton on burlap. Early twentieth century. 15" x 22". *Courtesy of Robin Moore Walker.*

Geese fly through a night sky above the tops of barely visible evergreen trees. Brin (jute) on burlap. Early twentieth century. 25" x 40". *Courtesy of Robin Moore Walker.*

In V formation, geese take flight over an illuminated forest. Cotton on burlap. Early twentieth century. 40" x 64". *Courtesy of Robin Moore Walker.*

A faithful sled dog is portrayed in this detailed hooked study. Rayon on burlap. 1940-1960. 14" x 12". *Courtesy of Robin Moore Walker.*

Complete with tipped tail, a friendly fox smiles at his audience. Brin (jute) and rayon on burlap. Early twentieth century. 6" x 7". *Courtesy of Robin Moore Walker.*

With head held high, a sled dog in harness surveys his lofty surroundings. Silk, rayon, and cotton on burlap. Early twentieth century. Diameter 8". *Courtesy of Robin Moore Walker.*

As snow falls, a deer nibbles on tender green leaves. Rayon on burlap. 1940-1960. 17" x 13". *Courtesy of Robin Moore Walker.*

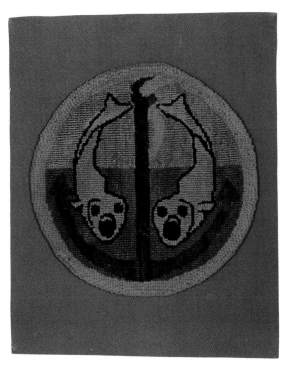

A map of Newfoundland is the backdrop to a lifelike replica of a leaping trout. Silk on burlap. Early twentieth century. 26" x 20". *Courtesy of Robin Moore Walker.*

An anchor separates two open-mouthed fish. Brin (jute) on burlap. Early twentieth century. Diameter 8". *Courtesy of Robin Moore Walker.*

Two walruses bask in the warmth of the Northern sun. Silk, rayon, and cotton on burlap. Early twentieth century. 25" x 38". *Courtesy of Robin Moore Walker.*

With faces hidden by their hoods, travelers make their way through deep snow. To create the "fur"-trimmed parkas, raised woolen yarn loops were clipped and fluffed with a stiff brush. Rayon on burlap with woolen yarns. 1940-1960. 11" x 18". *Courtesy of Robin Moore Walker.*

Two interpretations of a gun-toting Inuit woman. Each mat maker expressed her own personal flair for fashion. Rayon on burlap. Both are early twentieth century and 9" x 7". *Courtesy of Robin Moore Walker.*

Red mittens warm the hands of an Inuit figure as he navigates his kayak between dangerous ice floes. Cotton on burlap. Early twentieth century. 21" x 36". *Courtesy of Robin Moore Walker.*

A well-padded Inuit woman (with rare facial features) is posed against a village setting. Rayon on burlap. Early twentieth century. 9" x 7". *Courtesy of Robin Moore Walker.*

A harbor scene composed of simple shapes is enhanced by a delicately shaded sky. Rayon and cotton on burlap. Early twentieth century. 22" x 27". *Courtesy of Robin Moore Walker.*

Brightly colored boats sail into the sunset as angular ice floes dot a darkened sea. Brin (jute) and cotton on burlap. Early twentieth century. 14" x 50". *Courtesy of Robin Moore Walker.*

Under full sail, a clipper ship cuts through turbulent waters. Cotton on burlap. Early twentieth century. 27" x 39". *Courtesy of Robin Moore Walker.*

The billowing black smoke of a
Labrador ice breaker melds into the
hooked frame of this one-of-a-kind
mat. Attributed to the Grenfell
Labrador Industries. Cotton, silk, and
rayon on burlap. Early twentieth
century. 13" x 20". *Courtesy of Robin
Moore Walker.*

As darkness approaches, lamplight
shines through windows and an open
door of this Northern home. Cotton,
rayon, and brin (jute) on burlap. Early
twentieth century. Diameter 6".
Courtesy of Robin Moore Walker.

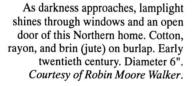

A hooked postcard view of St.
Anthony, Newfoundland. Goats and a
cow graze near a winding path that
leads to a distant lighthouse. Silk and
rayon on burlap. Early twentieth
century. 27" x 39". *Courtesy of Robin
Moore Walker.*

Plump birds fly over a sunny church-yard setting as a goat enters the scene. Cotton and brin (jute) on burlap. Early twentieth century. 22" x 27". *Courtesy of Robin Moore Walker.*

In addition to the popular Northern scenes, the Grenfell Labrador Industries offered hooked mats of colorful floral patterns. Rayon on burlap. Early twentieth century. 30" x 40". *Courtesy of Robin Moore Walker.*

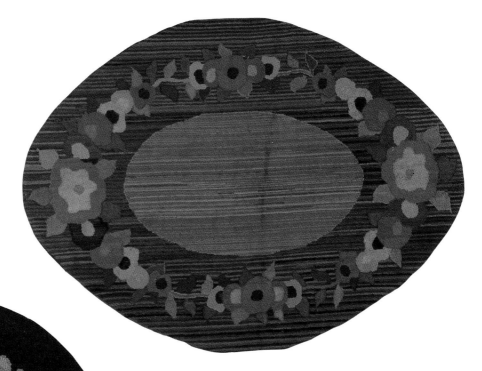

Native flowers and foliage are pictured on this tabletop mat. Cotton, silk, and rayon on burlap. Early twentieth century. Diameter 14". *Courtesy of Robin Moore Walker.*

4. Rugs on Exhibit

Old York Historical Society

In 1898, Miss Elizabeth Perkins (1869-1952) and her mother, Mary Sowles Perkins, purchased the "Piggin House" on the York River in the Piscataqua Region of Maine. The eighteenth-century Colonial Revival home was to be their summer residence. Under the watchful eyes of the new owners, the structure underwent restoration and refurbishment. To enhance the interior, mother and daughter began acquiring hooked rugs, mainly to cover bedroom floors. Their collection of more than fifty rugs was purchased from suppliers in Kentucky, Virginia, and Nova Scotia as well as from local merchants.

The Perkins House and its contents were bequeathed to the town of York upon the death of Miss Elizabeth in 1952.

During the summer of 1994, newly appointed curator Thomas Johnson presented "Hooked Rugs from the Collections of the Old York Historical Society." The showing of twenty-three selected rugs was held at Maine's oldest surviving public building, the Old Gaol in York. On display were several of the hooked rugs collected by Elizabeth and Mary Perkins. In conjunction with the exhibit, members of the Seacoast Ruggers, a local rug-hooking organization, demonstrated their time-honored craft.

In 1898, Miss Elizabeth Perkins (1869-1952) and her mother, Mary Sowles Perkins, purchased an eighteenth-century house on the York River in the Piscataqua Region of Maine. After the summer home was restored, mother and daughter began to purchase hooked rugs. Pictured in the Perkins House are some of the rugs from their collection.

Hit-or-miss stripes of color play host to a simple array of flowers. Early twentieth century. The Perkins House. *Courtesy of the Old York Historical Society, York, Maine.*

The Seacoast Ruggers, a local rug hooking organization, reproduced a faithful likeness of the original stair runner used by Elizabeth Perkins and her mother. Presented to the Old York Historical Society, the hooked runner is now in place at the Perkins House. *Courtesy of the Old York Historical Society, York, Maine.*

An area-size hooked rug of basket-weave pattern graces a bedroom floor of this historical home. Early twentieth century. The Perkins House. *Courtesy of the Old York Historical Society, York, Maine.*

Brightly colored tumbling blocks are controlled by a Greek key border. Rows of braiding were sewn to decorate and protect the rug's edges. Early twentieth century. The Perkins House. *Courtesy of the Old York Historical Society, York, Maine.*

Autumn's red leaves surround an oval wreath of summer blossoms. Early twentieth century. The Perkins House. *Courtesy of the Old York Historical Society, York, Maine.*

Located in York, the Old Gaol is Maine's oldest surviving public building. During the summer of 1994, the historical landmark housed an exhibit entitled "Hooked Rugs from the Collection of the Old York Historical Society." *Courtesy of the Old York Historical Society, York, Maine.*

A gallery view of the hooked rugs on display at the Old Gaol. *Courtesy of the Old York Historical Society, York, Maine.*

Age has softened the colors and textures of this charming hooked bouquet in a basket. A braided border was sewn to the rug. Hooked on linen. 1870-1890. 35" x 48". *Courtesy of the Old York Historical Society, York, Maine.*

Named for the coastal Maine town where they purportedly originated, Waldoboro-type hooked rugs are characterized by raised pile designs. Pictured is a fine example of an ornate floral display with a raised central wreath. Believed to have been purchased by Miss Perkins or her mother. From the Perkins House. 1910-1930. 32" x 60". *Courtesy of the Old York Historical Society, York, Maine.*

Intricate scrollwork frames simple sprays of stylized and raised flowers. Waldoboro-type. Believed to have been purchased by Miss Perkins or her mother. From the Perkins House. 1910-1930. 29" x 50". *Courtesy of the Old York Historical Society, York, Maine.*

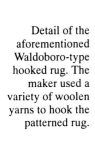

Detail of the aforementioned Waldoboro-type hooked rug. The maker used a variety of woolen yarns to hook the patterned rug.

A lively rug of traditional design and bold color. 1920-1940. 28" x 52". *Courtesy of the Old York Historical Society, York, Maine.*

The combination of roses and scrolls was a popular hooked rug pattern. Waldoboro-type with raised floral center. Believed to have been purchased by Miss Perkins or her mother. From the Perkins House. 1910-1930. 32" x 62". *Courtesy of the Old York Historical Society, York, Maine.*

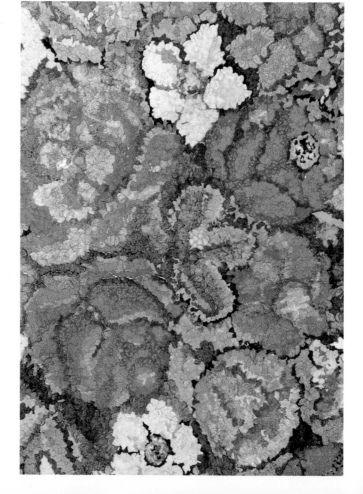

The use of vibrant colors, as shown in this detail of the aforementioned rug, gives a timeless quality to the composition.

Scrolls in outline form surround a
colorful spray of flowers and foliage.
The center trio of roses is raised.
Waldoboro-type. 1910-1930. 23" x 42".
*Courtesy of the Old York Historical
Society, York, Maine.*

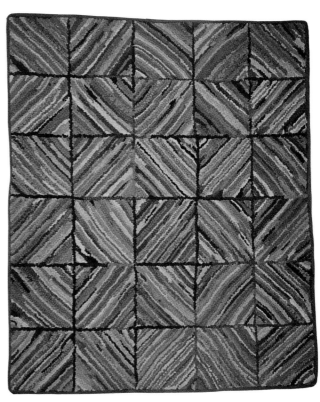

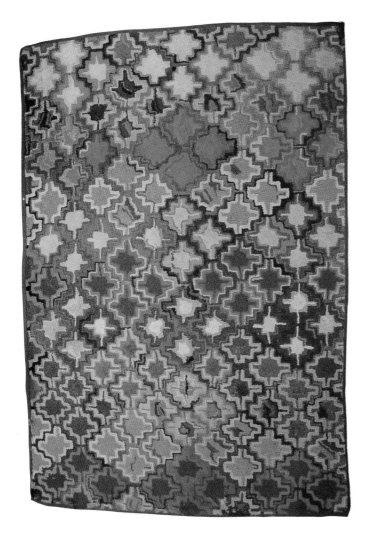

Hit-or-miss stripes of color, contained
in a black-line grid, form an intriguing
optical illusion. Purchased by Miss
Perkins. 1920-1940. 35" x 40".
*Courtesy of the Old York Historical
Society, York, Maine.*

When selecting hooked rugs, Miss
Perkins purchased several geometric
patterns including this multicolored
stepped diamond design. 1920-1940.
30" x 45". *Courtesy of the Old York
Historical Society, York, Maine.*

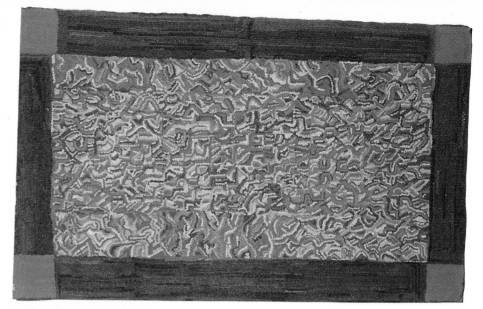

This rug of an abstract field framed in black is very similar in design to earlier Shaker-made hooked-type rugs. 1920-1940. 30" x 51". *Courtesy of the Old York Historical Society, York, Maine.*

Composed of conch shells, hearts, and a central five-pointed star, this nautical-motif rug reported to be of York, Maine, origins, was perhaps hooked by the wife or bride-to-be of a seafaring man, if not the man himself. 1870-1890. 37" x 38". *Courtesy of the Old York Historical Society, York, Maine.*

With childlike disregard for perspective, the end gables of this stately home have been flattened to occupy the same visual plane as the structure's facade. Striped patterns overhead and on each side of the house create an almost vibrating motion. 1880-1900. 31" x 30". *Courtesy of the Old York Historical Society, York, Maine.*

A frame of multicolored triangles enhances a trio of "fancy" diamonds. 1910-1930. 22" x 35". *Courtesy of the Old York Historical Society, York, Maine.*

Rosalie Lent, a member of Seacoast Ruggers, demonstrates the art of rug hooking at the Old Gaol. *Courtesy of Rosalie Lent and the Old York Historical Society, York, Maine.*

An unsophisticated image of a trotting horse, reminiscent of weathervane forms of the period, was placed upon a background which, like the wind, is ever changing. 1880-1900. 26" x 47". *Courtesy of the Old York Historical Society, York, Maine.*

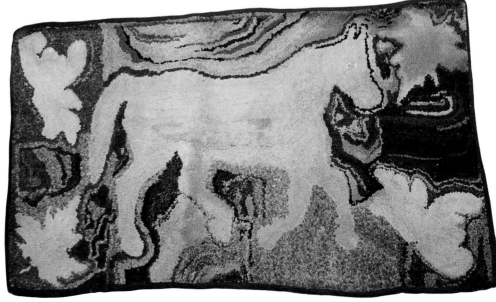

Colors of the American Southwest enrich Frost's Turkish Pattern #132. 1920-1940. 23" x 42". *Courtesy of the Old York Historical Society, York, Maine.*

The maker of this rug took artistic liberties with Edward Sands Frost's Turkish Pattern #108. Frost (1843-1894), a native of Maine, designed and sold preprinted hooked rug patterns after the Civil War. When poor health made a move to California necessary, Frost sold his pattern business to the Mayor of Biddeford, Maine. Reprints of the popular Frost designs are available to modern-day rug hookers. It is likely that this rug was purchased locally by Miss Perkins for her summer home on the York River. 1890-1910. 28" x 53". *Courtesy of the Old York Historical Society, York, Maine.*

This room-size composition of summer's bounty was designed and worked over four years by York's noted rug hooker, Anna Ketzler. Using all hand-dyed woolen fabrics, the master rug maker fashioned a central medallion of grapes and leaves framed by fruited borders of melons, strawberries, grapes, blackberries, apples, pears, and peaches. The rug and its creator were featured in the 1950 winter issue of *New England Living* magazine. Sarah Newick of York, whose mother was a student of Mrs. Ketzler's, generously added the impressive rug to the Historical Society's collection. 1947-1951. 7' 3" x 8' 9". *Courtesy of the Old York Historical Society, York, Maine.*

Opposite page:
A detail of Anna Ketzler's hooked rug reveals a full palette of rich colors and documentation of the year the room-size project was started.

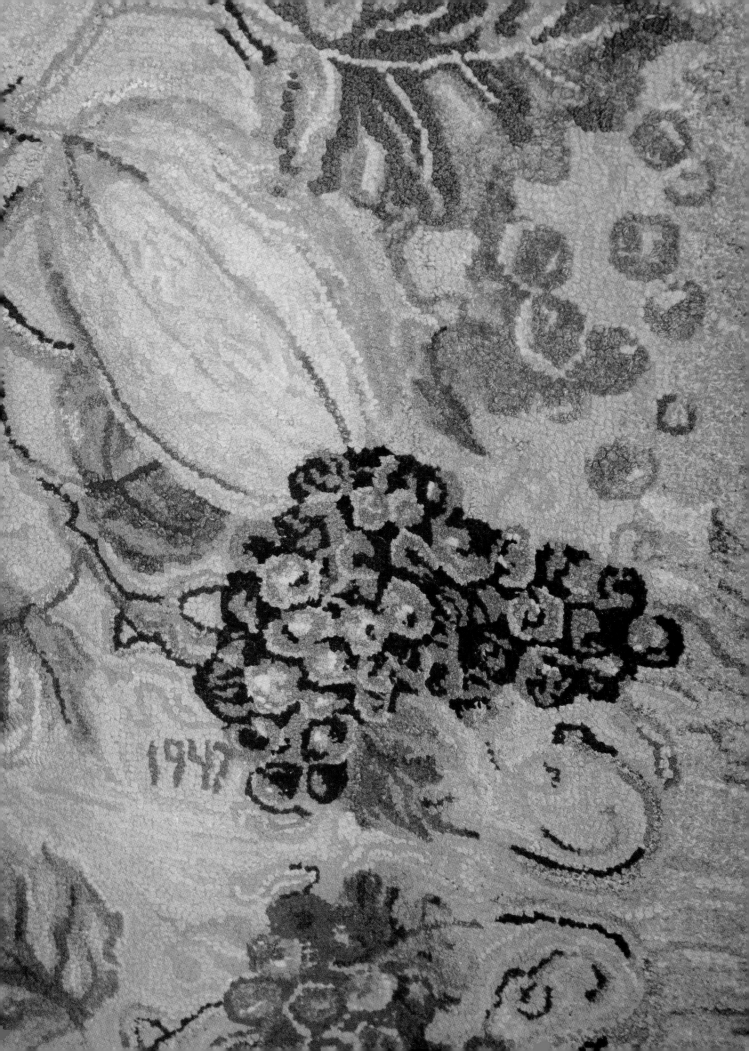

"Northern Scenes: Hooked Art of the Grenfell Mission" and "Silk Stocking Mats"

Two traveling exhibits of Grenfell mats and related items toured the United States and Canada from February 1994 through October 1996. The hooked mats on exhibit depicted Northern scenes crafted in Newfoundland and Labrador during the first forty years of this century. The two shows were made possible by guest curator Paula Laverty, contributing collectors, and museums and galleries sponsoring the events. Tour stops included the Museum of American Folk Art in New York City, the Shelburne Museum in Vermont, Memorial University of Newfoundland in St. John's, the Curtis Memorial Hospital Gallery in St. Anthony, Newfoundland, and North West River in Labrador.

The Museum of American Folk Art in New York City was the first to host "Northern Scenes: Hooked Art of the Grenfell Missions," a traveling exhibit. *Courtesy of Paula Laverty.*

Decorative as well as functional, this hooked book cover, included in the exhibit, is exemplary of the ingenuity shown by those who worked for the Grenfell Labrador Industries. 1920-1940. 10" x 15". *Courtesy of Patricia Smith.*

"Fish on Flake" was among the mats on display. The distinctive design was inspired by racks of codfish that were left to dry in the Northern sun. 1930s. *Courtesy of the Collection of Paula and Bill Laverty.*

The traveling exhibit of Grenfell art made a tour stop at Memorial University of Newfoundland in St John's. *Courtesy of Paula Laverty.*

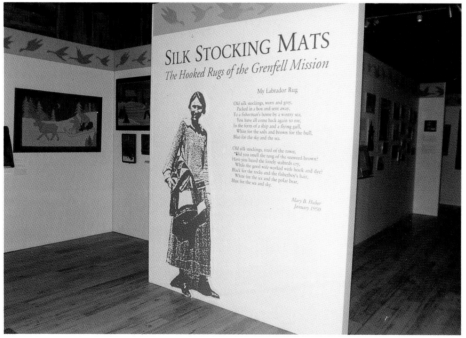

Vermont's Shelburne Museum welcomed "Silk Stocking Mats." *Courtesy of Paula Laverty.*

"Hooked on the Sea"

Ralph E. Cahoon (1910-1982) was an American painter known for his whimsical sea-related scenes. When the Cahoon Museum of American Art, former home of Cahoon and his artist wife Martha, sponsored a juried competition for all rug hookers entitled "Hooked on the Sea," the response was overwhelming. The subject was nautical. The medium was anything hooked. Entries arrived at the steps of the Cotuit, Massachusetts, museum from across the United States, Canada, and Japan.

Under the guidance of curator Peg Irish, the exhibit opened in June and ran through September 1995, attracting one of the largest audiences the small but popular Cape Cod museum had ever seen. Featured were nearly forty contemporary hooked pieces of original design, complemented by vintage and antique hooked rugs of nautical theme.

Exterior view of the Cahoon Museum of American Art, former home of artists Ralph and Martha Cahoon, in Cotuit, Massachusetts. *Courtesy of the Cahoon Museum of American Art.*

"Cape Knitting Company" by Ralph Cahoon (1910-1982). *Courtesy of the Cahoon Museum of American Art.*

"Young Mermaid in Red with Her Catfish," designed and hooked by Pat Merikallio of Connecticut, was awarded best-in-show and was used by the museum to advertise the exhibition "Hooked on the Sea". The rug was inspired by two American folk paintings. 31" x 37". *Courtesy of Pat Merikallio.*

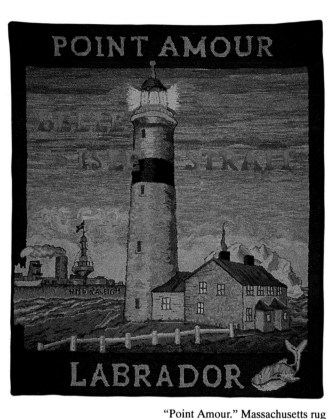

"Point Amour." Massachusetts rug hooking artist Joan Stocker recalls with hook and wool the lighthouse that guided seven hundred shipwrecked sailors to safety off the coast of Newfoundland and Labrador in 1922. 38" x 32". *Courtesy of Joan M. Stocker.*

"Oceanic Fantasy." Catherine Clay of Massachusetts ventures into uncharted tropical waters, creating her first original design with splendid results. 31" x 45". *Courtesy of Catherine Clay.*

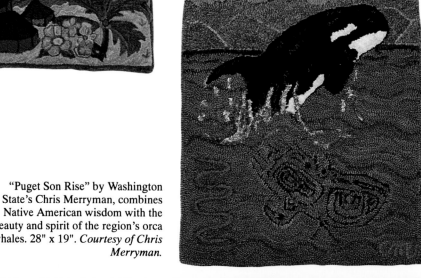

"Puget Son Rise" by Washington State's Chris Merryman, combines Native American wisdom with the beauty and spirit of the region's orca whales. 28" x 19". *Courtesy of Chris Merryman.*

This rug is the second of what Mrs. Supple calls her "grandmother series," made with the help of her grandson Richard, who is an enthusiastic visitor at the New England Aquarium in Boston, Massachusetts. He helped his grandmother choose which fish would swim in the waters of her "Caribbean Coral Reef." 27" x 35". *Courtesy of Elizabeth A. Supple.*

"Mermaids' Washday." Invited by the museum to participate in the exhibit, C. Lois Dugal of New Hampshire replicated a Ralph Cahoon painting using actual pearls to enhance the beauty of her hooked work. 27" x 21". *Courtesy of C. Lois Dugal.*

Born in the Caribbean and now living in Massachusetts, world traveler Jacqueline Gutting captures sea, surf, and moonlight in "Clair de Lune Tropical." 25" x 37". *Courtesy of Jacqueline Denizard Gutting.*

The pictured "Sailor's Star" was made by a New England-based mariner during the mid 1800s. Short lengths of cotton thread were bunched, tied, and then sewn onto a canvas sailcloth. Though not of the hooked variety, this rug is exemplary of needlework done by seafaring men. 22" x 46". The small mat depicting a sailboat was hooked by mat makers working for the Grenfell Labrador Industries. Early twentieth century. 8" x 9".

"Sea Cache." "Where the land and sea meet are the 'treasures of the past: pirate loot, ships lost at sea and remains of Nature's creatures.'" So describes Connecticut-based Trudi Shippenberg's three-panel wall hanging. 36" x 72". *Courtesy of Trudi Shippenberg.*

Maryland's noted rug hooking artist Mary Sheppard Burton recalls frozen riverfront family histories in her well-regarded "Tell Me 'Bout Series— #1 When Pa Was Young—Skating the Bay." 68" x 45". *Courtesy Mary Sheppard Burton.*

Homage is paid to nineteenth-century poet and gardener Celia Thaxter by Massachusetts rug hooker Elizabeth Green. This tiny garden survives the harsh conditions of the Isles of Shoals, off the New Hampshire coast. In the poet's words, "Now is the garden at the high tide of beauty." 25" x 18". *Courtesy of Elizabeth T. Green.*

The "Seawitch" was adapted from a painting by an unknown British artist. Marcy Van Roosen of North Carolina has pictured the brig rounding the Isle of White. 28" x 38". *Courtesy of Marcy Van Roosen.*

Another in the fascinating "Tell Me 'Bout Series— #2 When Pa Was Young—The Tool Fetcher" by Mary Sheppard Burton. Pa retrieved the dropped tools of laborers working to build a bridge across the cold Susquehanna River. 32" x 46". *Courtesy of Mary Sheppard Burton.*

"Icescape" was meticulously crafted by Gloria Crouse of Washington State using various hooking tools and variety of white materials. 60" x 60". *Courtesy of Gloria E. Crouse.*

Taking a feline approach to a beloved nursery rhyme about three wise men in a bowl, Massachusetts' own Jeanie Crockett Ritchie adds a whimiscal touch to a nautical theme. 34" x 39". *Courtesy Jean Crockett Ritchie.*

"Historic Nantucket—Scrimshawed." Carolyn Watt of Massachusetts celebrates the island of Nantucket and its relationship to the sea. 24" x 38". *Courtesy of Carolyn Arrington-Watt.*

The subject matter for "Clam Shells to Rainbows" sprang from various sources. Esther Jackson of Rhode Island and Florida chose to combine her passion for quilting and shell collecting with the illustrations from a children's nonsense poem. 28" x 25". *Courtesy of Esther R. Jackson.*

Nevada's D. Marie Bresch dedicated "Images of the Sea" to her husband's thirty years of naval service. Diameter 30". *Courtesy of D. Marie Bresch.*

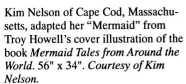

Kim Nelson of Cape Cod, Massachusetts, adapted her "Mermaid" from Troy Howell's cover illustration of the book *Mermaid Tales from Around the World.* 56" x 34". *Courtesy of Kim Nelson.*

Charlene Marsh of Indiana has hooked a searing environmental statement protesting the abandonment of fishnets in our seas. "Driftnets." 62" x 91". *Courtesy of Charlene Marsh, copyright 1991.*

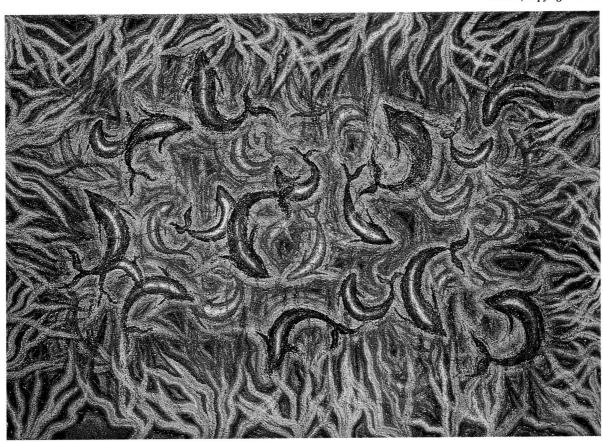

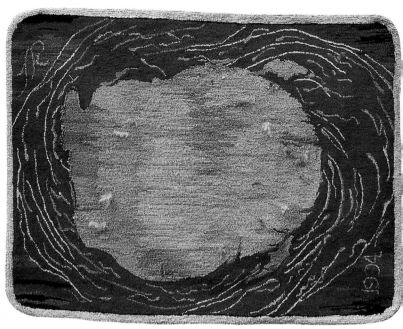

"Bay of the Mermaids" by Jean Jones of Massachusetts, is an enchanting portrait of frolicking mermaids and friendly sea creatures. 34" x 34". *Courtesy of Jean L. Jones.*

What better way than mixed media to depict the "Sargasso Sea," the mysterious golden sea "composed of thatch, seaweed, and anything that floats." Florence Richardson-Rich of Cape Cod, Massachusetts. 36" x 48". *Courtesy of Florence Richardson-Rich.*

Whales' tails, currents, and waves frame a scene of sea and shore. The inspiration for "Justin's Whale Rug," by Jule Marie Smith of New York, was a whale-watching expedition off Provincetown, Massachusetts. 36" x 60". *Courtesy of Jule Marie Smith.*

In addition to the juried exhibits, the Cahoon Museum of American Art offered other hooked rugs of nautical interest. Displayed above the sea chest is "Capturing a Sperm Whale," a hooked reproduction of an aquatint engraving. The artist, Virginia Sheldon, has previously had her work shown at the Kendall Whaling Museum in her hometown of Sharon, Massachusetts. 1981. 35" x 52". The scenic panel on the opposite wall, "Newburyport, Massachusetts from Salisbury" was hooked in the early 1990s by Theresa Wells, also of Massachusetts. 29" x 60". The old Ralph Burnham pattern portrays the Atlantic coastline town during 1847, when the harbor was a bustling center for seafaring activities. Burnham, during the turn of the century until his death in 1938, sold choice hooked rugs to a prestigious clientele. From his Ipswich, Massachusetts, Trading Post, he also provided expert repair services and a complete line of ready-to-hook rug patterns. Burnham's wife, Nellie, continued the pattern business until 1958. Interestingly, Ms. Wells is a student of Annie Spring who is Ralph Burnham's neice. On loan to the museum for this exhibit, courtesy of Ms. Spring, was an original copy of the burlap rug pattern, "Newburyport, Massachusetts, from Salisbury." *Courtesy of Virginia Sheldon, Theresa J. Wells, and Annie A. Spring.*

Inspired by her father's painting, Olga Rothschild of Massachusetts hooked from recylced wool "Landeck's Fish," the study of a sea bass caught off Cape Cod waters. 30" x 40". *Courtesy of Olga Rothschild.*

The "Hooked on the Sea" juried exhibit attracted the attention of rug hookers worldwide, including that of Japanese artist Fumiyo Hachisuka. Placed opposite "Landeck's Fish" is "Stroll in the Sea," a scene of underwater activity captured in diverse colors. Often working with discarded silk kimonos, Fumiyo learned to hook rugs in Canada, where her husband was stationed for an eight-year work assignment. Currently residing in Tokyo, she exhibits her work, teaches the craft, and spreads the joy of rug hooking in a land where very little is known about this North American art. 60" x 36". *Courtesy of Fumiyo Hachisuka.*

"Allegra," based on Martha Cahoon's painting "Skylark," was hooked by invited participant and Cape Cod resident Shirley Wiedemann. Making note of her and her husband's Scandinavian heritage, Norwegian and Swedish flags adorn the central hot air balloon named for the Wiedemann's boat. 36" x 24". *Courtesy of Shirley Wiedemann.*

Fashioned after an antique rug with a borrowed quilt pattern border, New York's Marilyn Bottjer added her own nautical touch of sporting whales, primping mermaids, and a verse from the John Donne poem "Song of the Sea." 39" x 50". *Courtesy of Marilyn Bottjer.*

Janet Stanley Reid, a native of Massachusetts now living in Pennsylvania for more than twenty years, credits annual visits to Cape Cod and the islands for the original spark which motivated her to hook "Home by the Sea." 26" x 36". *Courtesy of Janet Stanley Reid.*

"Yes, pelicans can be seen in Kansas, if only briefly in the wetland preserves during their spring migration. Their brief time in the Midwest is only bearable due to the sheer multitude of pelicans that gather in the hundreds—a wonderful sight!" Loretta Schuster of Kansas, a Hallmark card artist for thirty years, was inspired by a favorite verse, "Pelican, pelican, whose beak can hold more than his belly can." 31" x 38". *Courtesy of Loretta M. Schuster.*

"The notion for this design came from a small, carved stone capital on the top of a cathedral column that I happened to see in a book about Medieval sculpture." In "Fisherman," painter and sculptress Marjorie Noon of New Hamphire has successfully combined three areas of interest—her love of sculpture, her dramatic use of color in her paintings, and her talents as a rug hooker. 36" x 48". *Courtesy of Marjorie Noon.*

"The shimmering waters, tall firs, and soaring mountains of the Pacific Northwest make it such a magnificent place to live that we tend to forget the totally different world that exists here—beneath the sea. The Seattle Aquarium has an underwater amphitheater where you are surrounded by local sea life. It is a mesmerizing place to spend time and this piece is the result," says Washington State's Chris Merryman of "Good Morning Puget Sound." 50" x 66". *Courtesy of Chris Merryman.*

Recalling her son's favorite childhood storybook, Patricia Haviland created "Gullport," a hooked adaptation of the dockside scene in *Kermit the Hermit*, by Bill Peet. The hooking artist is a Massachusetts resident. 32" x 39". *Courtesy of Patricia Haviland.*

"People and Places"

A one-woman show of Roslyn Logsdon's hooked art was held at the Montpelier Cultural Arts Center in Laurel, Maryland, during November 1996. The painter-turned-rug-hooking-artist drew upon her experiences with European travel to present "People and Places," a series of hooked vignettes capturing special moments and scenes. The work exhibited was completed over a period of two years, November 1994 through October 1996.

"November in Paris," as seen through bare branches. Roslyn Logsdon. 25" x 39". *Courtesy of Roslyn Logsdon.*

A canine friend patiently waits by the door of a "Medieval Abbey." Roslyn Logsdon. 29" x 36". *Courtesy of Roslyn Logsdon.*

"Garden Wall." Solid blocks of stone offer life to delicate flower and foliage. Roslyn Logsdon. 13" x 17". *Courtesy of Roslyn Logsdon.*

"Firenze." In contrast to buildings of age-softened tones, vibrant modern signs restrict traffic from entering a narrow street in Florence. Roslyn Logsdon. 35" x 23". *Courtesy of Roslyn Logsdon.*

"When I Was Seventeen." A relaxed self-portrait of the artist in her teenage years. Roslyn Logsdon. 14" x 22". *Courtesy of Roslyn Logsdon.*

Perhaps the seated gentleman in the "Cafe-by-the-Window" has just realized his *faux pas* concerning the unknown party who has left the table, with glass of wine unfinished. Roslyn Logsdon. 17" x 26". *Courtesy of Roslyn Logsdon.*

A "Woman in the Window" gazes out as we gaze in. Roslyn Logsdon. 20" x 17". *Courtesy of Roslyn Logsdon.*

A trio of friends gather for a relaxing moment. "Vins des Rues I."
Roslyn Logsdon. 31" x 21". *Courtesy of Roslyn Logsdon.*

A moment of solitude would be enjoyed on the "Bench by the Garden
Wall." Roslyn Logsdon. 20" x 15". *Courtesy of Roslyn Logsdon.*

"Vins des Rues II," from a different point of view. Roslyn Logsdon.
21" x 19". *Courtesy of Roslyn Logsdon.*

No matter where you travel, people-watching is always a popular
pastime. "Jolly Caffe." Roslyn Logsdon. 34" x 27". *Courtesy of
Roslyn Logsdon.*

5. Rugs at Auction

Hooked rug collections are accumulated in a variety of ways. Those with an abundance of time, talent, and fabrics can create their own hooked treasures. Enthusiasts eager to start a collection of new hooked rugs but not willing to do the work can buy, barter, or commission hooked pieces. Vintage and antique hooked rugs may be purchased, traded, or inherited. Occasionally these old hooked rugs can be found in antique shops and at shows, flea markets, estate sales, and auctions. The demand for choice hooked rugs, antique or modern, has always been greater than the supply.

Those few hooked rugs that go up for auction tend to take a back seat to their Oriental carpet cousins unless they are exceptional or part of a well-known collection. Rarely is an entire auction agenda devoted to hooked rugs.

Anderson Galleries
New York City, 1923

At 2:30 in the afternoon, May 9-10, 1923, the Anderson Galleries of Park Avenue and 59th Street in New York City offered for sale at auction the "Hook Rugs" of Mr. James E. Shoemaker of Manhasset, Long Island. The collection of two hundred and ninety-five rugs had been gathered over the previous fifteen years. Designs and ages were varied. Sizes ranged from small mats to room-size floor coverings. Many of the rugs sold during the two-day event became important additions to other hooked rug collections, including those of Ralph Burnham and William Winthrop Kent.

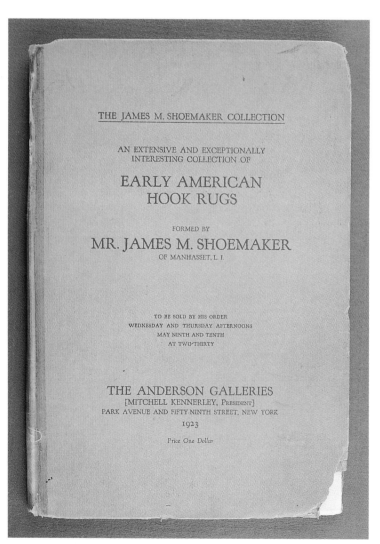

An auction catalog from 1923, complete with descriptions and photographs of Mr. Shoemaker's "Early American Hook Rugs," was offered to interested buyers for one dollar.

Reprints from Pages 24 and 25 of the catalog describe a variety of the hooked rugs to be auctioned. The pictured duck and patriotic designs were hooked from popular patterns printed on burlap and sold by Edward Sands Frost in the late 1860s. Burlap was first imported and introduced into the North American region during the 1850s. This author therefore questions the ascribed age as being Early American. Throughout the catalog the vintages assigned to many of the hooked rugs tend to be rather generous.

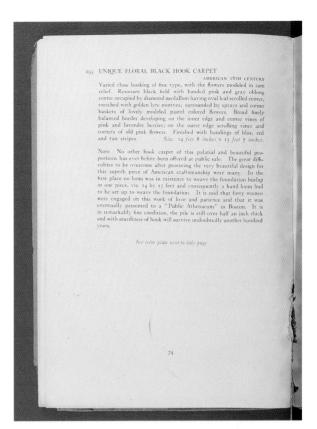

Reserved for the auction catalog's only color plate was a hooked rug
of grand proportions and illustrious heritage, reported to be the finest
in Mr. Shoemaker's collection. Description reprinted from Page 74.
Reported age is questionable.

[211]

The reprint of Page 41
from the auction catalog
offers descriptions of
another select group of Mr.
Shoemaker's hooked rugs.
This author questions the
ascribed ages that
accompany each rug.

211 MODELED LAMBSWOOL HOOKED RUG

AMERICAN CIRCA 1820
Deep close hooking. Ivory field sustaining close oval bouquet of
ivory, yellow, lavender and red flowers very finely modeled. Unique
border of trailing grapes and vines similarly modeled and inter-
rupted at corners with large leaf motives.
Size: 4 feet 5 inches x 2 feet 1 inch.
[ILLUSTRATED]

212 INSCRIBED MEDALLION HOOK RUG AMERICAN CIRCA 1820
Field occupied by large tan oval medallion, centered with jaspé blue
oblong displaying formal red bouquet and inscription "Mary Jane."
Tan corners developing pastel colored sprays of roses.
Size: 4 feet 5 inches x 2 feet 5 inches.

213 RARE ARCHED "WELCOME" HOOK RUG

AMERICAN CIRCA 1800
Arched dull-blue field; occupied by rosebush bearing large wine-
red blossoms and bud; below "Welcome" in black. Narrow black
borders. *Size: 3 feet 4 inches x 1 foot 11 inches.*

214 FLORAL TIGER SKIN HOOK RUG EARLY AMERICAN
Golden-tan field; marked with black simulating an animal's pelt;
occupied by a diamond medallion bearing blue lilies and enclosing
bouquet of crimson flowers.
Size: 2 feet 10 inches x 1 foot 10 inches.

41

Kaminski Auctioneers and Appraisers
Stoneham, Massachusetts, 1995

The summer air may have been still, but the bidding certainly wasn't, at the Kaminski auction held August 11, 1995, in the Massachusetts north shore seacoast community of Rockport. Offered for sale were more than a hundred hooked rugs acquired during the 1930s, '40s and '50s by a prominent antique dealer from Boston's tony Charles Street district. The rugs were of varying vintages and di-

mensions. In the collection were early hooked rugs on linen, rugs of original design, plus some worked from popular patterns of the time. Additions to the auction included Grenfell mats and a painstakingly hooked but yet-to-be-finished room-size rug. The auction did include other items such as furniture and china, but the audience was there to buy rugs. And buy they did.

The advance auction notice offers an enticing array of antique hooked rugs. *Courtesy of Kaminski Auctioneers and Appraisers.*

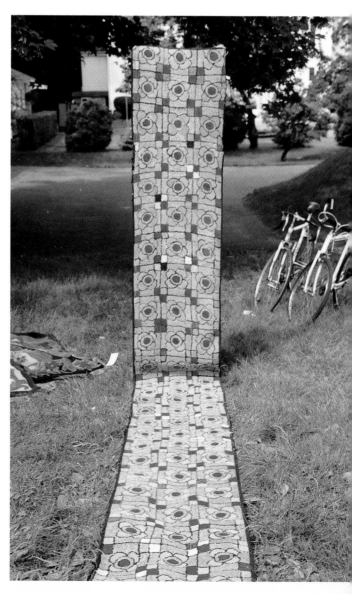

A lengthy runner of cheerful nature. Mixed materials on burlap. 1910-1930. 17' x 24". In need of repair. Sold for $412. *Courtesy of Kaminski Auctioneers and Appraisers.*

Subtly shaded scrollwork frames a wreath of rose blossoms, buds, and foliage. Floral sprays flank the central motif. Woolen fabrics hooked on burlap. Late nineteenth century. 31" x 60". Sold for $880. *Courtesy of Kaminski Auctioneers and Appraisers.*

Repeat geometrical pattern of medallions and diamonds. Mixed materials on burlap. Early twentieth century. 90" x 45". Sold for $550. *Courtesy of Kaminski Auctioneers and Appraisers.*

A finely hooked rug of flowers and scrolls. Woolen yarns on burlap. Early twentieth century. 28" x 56". Sold for $566. *Courtesy of Kaminski Auctioneers and Appraisers.*

An unusual Waldoboro-type hooked rug with raised and shirred grapes, berries, and central rose motif. Woolen yarns on burlap. Early twentieth century. 30" x 60". Sold for $522. *Courtesy of Kaminski Auctioneers and Appraisers.*

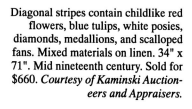

Diagonal stripes contain childlike red flowers, blue tulips, white posies, diamonds, medallions, and scalloped fans. Mixed materials on linen. 34" x 71". Mid nineteenth century. Sold for $660. *Courtesy of Kaminski Auctioneers and Appraisers.*

Topsy-turvy leaves frame duplicate bouquets of bold design. Mixed materials on burlap. Late nineteenth century. 37" x 66". Sold for $770. *Courtesy of Kaminski Auctioneers and Appraisers.*

This charming rug of bunnies, cats, kittens, and springtime daisies would delight any child. Cotton materials and woolen yarns on burlap. Early twentieth century. Scatter-size. Stained and in need of repair. Sold for $550. *Courtesy of Kaminski Auctioneers and Appraisers.*

Twin floral sprays of dynamic proportions create a lively rug. Mixed materials on burlap. Late nineteenth century. 38" x 68". Sold for $1,320. *Courtesy of Kaminski Auctioneers and Appraisers.*

A hexagon chain separates a pattern of cut flowers. Mixed materials on burlap. Late nineteenth century. 38" x 82". Sold for $990. *Courtesy of Kaminski Auctioneers and Appraisers.*

Vibrant colors were used to hook this pattern of twisting and turning scrolls. Early twentieth century. Woolen yarns on burlap. 53" x 90". Sold for $550. *Courtesy of Kaminski Auctioneers and Appraisers.*

Stars and hearts enhance a pair of wedding ring pattern hooked rugs. Mixed materials on burlap. Late nineteenth century. The rug pictured was 51" x 85" and sold for $1,430. The other half of the pair (not pictured) was of identical color and design. Dated 1896. 47" x 95". Sold for $990. *Courtesy of Kaminski Auctioneers and Appraisers.*

The image of a beloved pet dog is portrayed in duplicate. Mixed materials on burlap. Early twentieth century. 41" x 74". In need of repair. Sold for $660. *Courtesy of Kaminski Auctioneers and Appraisers.*

A braided edge decorates and protects this area-size tile pattern hooked rug. Mixed materials on burlap. Early twentieth century. 52" x 87". Sold for $1,210. *Courtesy of Kaminski Auctioneers and Appraisers.*

An eye-catching design of brightly colored plumes. Woolen yarns on burlap. Early twentieth century. 71" x 62". Sold for $990. *Courtesy of Kaminski Auctioneers and Appraisers.*

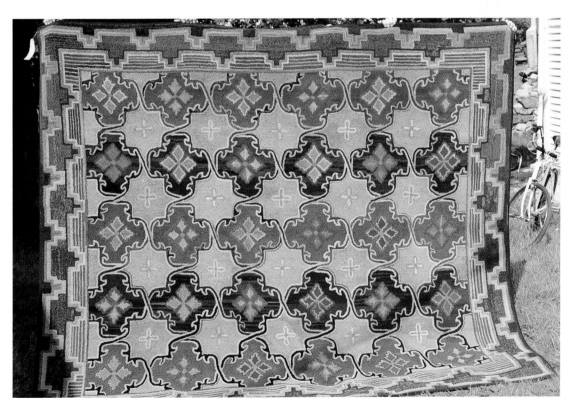

In excellent condition, this room-size rug of a medallion-design interior edged by varying borders was the subject of frenzied bidding. Mixed materials on burlap. Early twentieth century. 8' 9" x 7' 4". Sold for $3,520. *Courtesy of Kaminski Auctioneers and Appraisers.*

Collins Auction Galleries

On May 27, 1995, the Collins Auction Galleries of Kennebunk, Maine, offered for sale at auction the estate of Nellie Batchelder. The Maine native was born in Limerick in 1870 and died in Sanford in 1953. A talented needlework artist, Nellie Batchelder was accomplished at sewing, crocheting, knitting, needlepoint, and quilting. She was also a collector of varied interests. On view at the auction were antique furniture, glass, china, decorative arts, Persian and Kashmir shawls, a grouping of appliquéd quilts, many of which were fashioned by Nellie Batchelder, and a choice selection of more than thirty floral and pictorial hooked rugs that she had collected.

This page from the Nellie Batchelder estate auction brochure offered a visual feast for the eyes of any textile collector. Among the items put up for sale were quilts, Persian and Kashmir shawls, and Oriental and hooked rugs. *Courtesy of Collins Auction Galleries.*

A corner detail of an outstanding hooked rug of animals, birds, and floral clusters on a free-form background. Pictured in the aforementioned brochure, the rug is to the lower left of the star quilt. Early twentieth century. 6' x 9'. *Courtesy of Collins Auction Galleries.*

An array of antique treaures rest upon a fanciful hooked rug of animals, houses, boats, and birds. Early twentieth century. Above the tall chest hangs a circular hooked rug of simple floral design. 1920-1940. Reprinted from the Nellie Batchelder estate auction brochure. *Courtesy of the Collins Auction Galleries.*

English carved oak tall case clock, pine slatback chair, hearth cat, trencher bowls, circular hooked rug, Ridgways Staffordshire platter, Ruby stained block pattern glass ware, West Troy pattern 3 gallon decorated stoneware jug, obsidian art glass vase, Chippendale maple tall chest, early marquetry box, nest of hand carved Chinese rosewood tables, pair of Federal andirons, Copeland Staffordshire tureen with ladle and pictorial hooked rug.

6. Antique Shows and Shops

Hooked rug connoisseurs wanting to start or add to a
collection may find frequenting antique shows and shops
to be a rewarding experience.

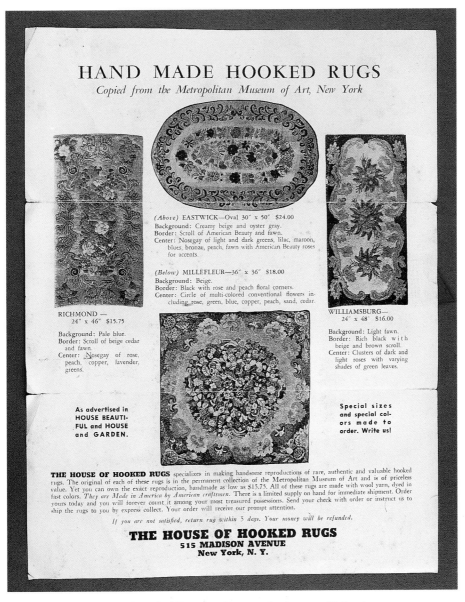

The House of Hooked Rugs lured prospective buyers with handsome
reproductions of "priceless" hooked rugs from the permanent
collection of New York's Metropolitan Museum of Art. Handbill
dates from 1910-1930.

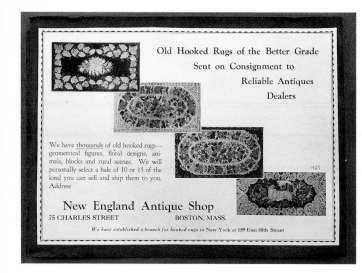

Available to clients on a trial basis, the New England Antique Shop of Boston offered a substantial inventory of old hooked rugs. From a magazine advertisement of an unknown source. Dated 1929. *Courtesy of Joan M. Stocker.*

Symbolic of "Good Luck," four red horseshoes are framed by stars and stripes. Late nineteenth century. 40" x 44". *Courtesy of Russ and Karen Goldberger.*

A late-nineteenth-century hooked rug of primitive potted flowers with a bold clamshell border was an attractive focal point in the booth of Russ and Karen Goldberger. New Hampshire Antique Dealers Show. Photo taken August 1995. *Courtesy of Russ and Karen Goldberger.*

Opposite page, top left: In addition to early country furniture and decorative arts, Colette Donovan offered patrons of this Wilton, Connecticut, antique show, sponsored by the Daughters of the American Revolution, a selection of fine antique hooked rugs, room-size to small tabletop mats. Displayed upon the wall is a late nineteenth century hooked-type rug attributed to the Shakers. Photo taken September 1996. *Courtesy of Colette Donovan.*

At Jim Burk's York, Pennsylvania, show, Russ and Karen Goldberger displayed a variety of choice antiques including this late nineteenth century hooked panel of four eight-pointed stars. Photo taken November 1995. *Courtesy of Russ and Karen Goldberger.*

Elizabeth Enfield exhibited an eclectic array of antique treasures. Select hooked rugs awaited eager customers. The Wilton Historical Society Annual Antique Show. Wilton, Connecticut. Photo taken March 1995. *Courtesy of Elizabeth Enfield/Mount Vernon Antiques.*

7. Hooked Rug Organizations

Throughout the United States and Canada, Europe and Asia, tens of thousands of women, men, and children continue to enjoy the tradition of hooking rugs. Many have come together to form rug hooking chapters that meet on a regular basis and promote their craft by sponsoring exhibits and workshops. The two largest rug hooking organizations in the United States are the McGown Guild and the Association of Traditional Hooking Artists (ATHA).

The roots of the McGown Guild were planted in the 1930s by rug hooking teacher and enthusiast Pearl McGown of West Boylston, Massachusetts. Currently the McGown Guild is headed by her granddaughter, Jane McGown Flynn, and numbers about two thousand members nationwide.

ATHA, founded in the New England region in 1979, boasts more than two thousand active members, including rug hookers across the United States, Canada, Japan, Australia, and Norway.

Farther north, the Ontario Hooking Craft Guild is Canada's largest organized group, with more than a thousand registered members. In May 1996, the guild celebrated its thirtieth anniversary with a three-day conference and exhibit in Toronto during which hundreds of rug hookers gathered to exchange ideas. Active in the Canadian Maritimes is the Rug Hooking Guild of Nova Scotia, with more than six hundred participants. Smaller groups can be found throughout Canada, including a newly organized chapter covering Newfoundland and Labrador.

The International Guild of Handhooking Rugmakers was formed to unite those all over the world who share a common love for hooking rugs. Their first seminar was held in England in 1994.

Rug hooking artist and teacher Hallie Hall started and completed "Aunt Harriet" during 1945. The room-size rug is a reproduction of an antique originally hooked by Harriet Fall Emery of Lebanon, Maine. With a passion for flowers and unlimited ambition, Mrs. Emery created an indoor hooked garden from the worn woolen clothing that she gathered and colored with natural dyes. For many years the prized rug was given a place of honor in the Emerys' Maine home. With the passing of both Mr. and Mrs. Emery, the once handsome rug, suffering from neglect, was relegated to the outdoor woodpile. A New York collector spotted the tattered hooked textile and purchased it in the early 1930s for $2,050. After undergoing $500 worth of repairs, the reclaimed rug was resold to B. Altman & Company of New York for $4,500. B. Altman & Company then sold it to the sister of a Southern governor. Reportedly, the rug eventually came into the possession of Vermont's Shelburne Museum. In 1935, rug hooking teacher Pearl McGown copied and sold the pattern after adjusting the design into an 8' x 12' oval. Pictured is Hallie Hall's unfinished "Aunt Harriet." *Courtesy of Hallie H. Hall.*

Hallie Hall's "Aunt Harriet" was the center of attraction at this 1945 hooked rug exhibit held in Long Island, New York. *Courtesy of Hallie H. Hall.*

A then twelve-year-old Jasmine Benjamin is pictured during the summer of 1992 with a sampling of her hooked handiwork. Jasmine is the daughter of Massachusetts designer and hooked rug teacher Jeanne Benjamin. In the five years since this photograph was taken, Jasmine has become a delightful young woman with several rug hooking awards to her credit. *Courtesy of Jeanne Benjamin.*

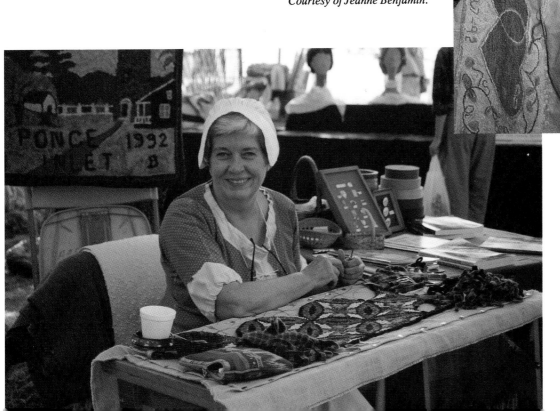

Dressed in period attire, rug hooking teacher Bettina Maraldo demonstrates her craft at Chadds Ford Days in Chadds Ford, Pennsylvania, in 1992. Ms. Maraldo resides in Florida. *Courtesy of Bettina Drake Maraldo.*

This New Hampshire Town Hall was the site of a well-attended
hooked rug exhibit in 1980. *Courtesy of Hallie H. Hall.*

The 1995 ATHA Biennial Exhibit was held in Arlington, Texas. Sandy Telzrow works on her latest hooked rug. *Courtesy of Cynthia Norwood.*

The Ontario Hooking Craft Guild of Canada celebrated its thirtieth anniversary by hosting a three-day conference and exhibit at the International Plaza in Toronto. Pictured is a small selection of the many hooked rugs that were on display. *Courtesy of the Ontario Hooking Craft Guild.*

Price Guide

The prices for hooked rugs have risen steadily over the past ten years. A growing appreciation by a widening audience has resulted in a demand for antique and contemporary hand-hooked rugs that is far greater than the supply.

A husband's daily request for his coffee was recorded for posterity by Massachusetts-based rug hooking teacher Jeanne Benjamin. 1995. 20" x 30". *Courtesy of Jeanne Benjamin.*

The cost to have a rug custom designed and hooked can vary from $50 per square foot to $300 per square foot. Price per square foot will be higher when commissioning rug hooking artists of note. Cost is affected by the complexity of the design, current price of woolen fabrics or other materials used, amount of hand-dyeing required, and width of the fabric strip the rug maker must hook with. The finer the strip is cut, the longer it takes to complete an area. When ordering a custom-made hooked rug, it is best to agree upon a per-square-foot fee before the project is started. Clients opting for being charged by the hour are often overwhelmed when it comes time to pay the bill. Few non-hookers are aware of the length of time necessary to hand craft a rug.

Unlike commissioned work, establishing a price guide for vintage and antique hooked rugs is difficult. The resale price for any hooked rug cannot be based on a per-square-foot fee. Those rugs coveted by collectors come with price tags that reflect their desirability. Early rugs hooked on linen are few and far between; prices generally begin around $500 and climb steadily from there. Antique hooked rugs with animal themes, that are aesthetically pleasing and that are in good condition, can start at $400, but have been known to exceed $20,000 at auction. Grenfell mats hooked in Newfoundland and Labrador during the early 1900s range in price from $200 to $8,000 depending upon subject matter, condition, and size. Expect to pay $3,000 and up for an older area or room-size hand-hooked rug in good condition. During the early months of 1997, an exceptional, room-size hooked rug that depicted dogs and dated from the late nineteenth century, reportedly sold at auction for $74,000.

Rugs hooked in the 1920s, 1930s, and after often cost less then their antique counterparts. The price range for these collectible rugs is wide. Bargains have been found for under $100, but it is not unrealistic to see prices reach into the thousands. Monetary values vary with demand, subject, age, size, and condition. Collectible hooked rugs are a good investment if carefully chosen and properly cared for.

Those who have not had experience buying rugs should be aware that all hooked rugs are not created equally. Due to their popularity, some carpet manufacturers advertise so called "hand-hooked" rugs for sale at low prices. Typically such rugs are actually machine made and mass produced. They do not have the appeal of a one-of-a-kind hand-crafted hooked rug and their value will not increase over time.

And then there are some of us who prefer tea. Betsy Adams. 1996. 21" x 28". *Courtesy of Betsy Adams.*

Bibliography

Books

Bowles, Ella Shannon. *Homespun Handicrafts.* Philadelphia: J.B. Lippincott Company, 1931.

Chiasson, Father Anselme, ed. *The History of Chéticamp Hooked Rugs and Their Artisans.* Yarmouth, Nova Scotia: Lescarbot Publications, 1988.

Gordon, Beverly. *Shaker Textile Arts.* Hanover, New Hampshire: The University Press of New England. 1980.

Kent, William Winthrop. *The Hooked Rug.* New York: Tudor Publishing Company, 1930.

Kent, William Winthrop. *Hooked Rug Design.* Springfield, Massachusetts: The Pond-Ekberg Company, 1949.

Kent, William Winthrop. *Rare Hooked Rugs.* Springfield, Massachusetts: The Pond-Ekberg Company, 1941.

Kopp, Joel and Kate. *American Hooked and Sewn Rugs.* New York: E. P. Dutton Inc., 1975.

Little, Nina Fletcher. *Little By Little.* New York, E. P. Dutton, Inc.: 1984.

McGown, Pearl K. *The Dreams Beneath Design.* Boston: Bruce Humphries, Inc., 1939.

Moshimer, Joan. *The Complete Rug Hooker.* Boston: New York Graphic Society, 1975.

Riznik, Barnes. *Waioli Mission House.* Lihue, Kauai, Hawaii: Grove Farm Homestead and Waioli Mission House, 1987.

Schleck, Robert, J. *The Wilcox Quilts in Hawaii.* Lihue, Kauai, Hawaii: Grove Farm Homestead and Waioli Mission House, 1986.

Sturges, Norma M. *The Braided Rug Book.* Asheville, North Carolina: Lark Books, 1995.

Tennant, Emma. *Rag Rugs of England and America.* London: Walker Books. 1992.

Turbayne, Jessie A. *Hooked Rugs: History and the Continuing Tradition.* West Chester, Pennsylvania: Schiffer Publishing Ltd. 1991.

Turbayne, Jessie A. *The Hooker's Art.* Atglen, Pennsylvania: Schiffer Publishing Ltd. 1993.

Waugh, Elizabeth and Edith Foley. *Collecting Hooked Rugs.* New York: The Century Co., 1927.

Articles

Author Unknown, "Barrington Woman Leads Way to Village Industries with Hope of Inspiring Neighbors in Creative Activities." *The Providence Sunday Journal Magazine* (August 25, 1929): 5.

Clancy, Jane, "Hawaiian Legacy." *Colonial Home* (August 1994): 72, 73, 74.

Cleveland, Debbie Regan, "Cogswell's Grant—The Littles' Place in the Country." *The New England Antiques Journal* (November 1994): 10, 55, 66.

Little, Nina Fletcher, "Antiques in Domestic Settings." *Antiques* magazine (June 1940): 292, 293.

Ruhland, Margaret, "George-Edouard Tremblay." *The Upper Canadian* (January/February 1989): 43.

Turim, Gayle, "Folk Art with a Stately Theme." *Americana* (February 1991): 38, 40.

Catalogues

American Classics—Hooked Rugs from the Barbara Johnson Collection. The Squibb Gallery. Princeton, New Jersey: December 22, 1988-January 29, 1989.

Hooked Rugs in the Folk Art Tradition. Museum of American Folk Art. New York: September 19-November 24, 1974.

Geometric patterns combine to create an optical illusion. Mixed materials including jute twine were used to create this graphic rug. Early twentieth century. 31" x 62". *Courtesy of Country Braid House.*

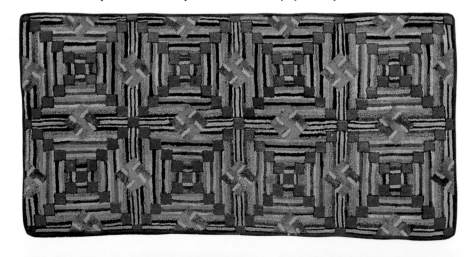